The Whole Gospel for the Whole World

McMaster Divinity College Press

McMaster Ministry Studies Series 3

LEADERSHIP *through* UNDERSTANDING

The Whole Gospel for the Whole World

Experiencing the Fourfold Gospel Today

FRANKLIN PYLES

AND

LEE BEACH

PICKWICK *Publications* • Eugene, Oregon

THE WHOLE GOSPEL FOR THE WHOLE WORLD
Experiencing the Fourfold Gospel Today

Mcmaster Ministry Studies Series 3

Mcmaster Divinity College Press
1280 Main Street West
Hamilton, Ontario, Canada
L8S 4K1

Pickwick Publications
An Imprint of Wipf and Stock Publishers
199 W. 8th Ave., Suite 3
Eugene, OR 97401

www.wipfandstock.com

PAPERBACK ISBN: 978-1-4982-9474-4
HARDCOVER ISBN: 978-1-4982-9476-8
EBOOK ISBN: 978-1-4982-9475-1

Cataloguing-in-Publication data:

Names: Pyles, Franklin. | Beach, Lee.

Title: The Whole Gospel for the Whole World : Experiencing the Fourfold Gospel Today / Franklin Pyles and Lee Beach.

Description: Eugene, OR: Pickwick Publications, 2016 | Series: Mcmaster Ministry Studies Series | Includes bibliographical references.

Identifiers: ISBN 978-1-4982-9474-4 (paperback) | ISBN 978-1-4982-9476-8 (hardcover) | ISBN 978-1-4982-9475-1 (ebook)

Subjects: LSCH: Christian and Missionary Alliance—Doctrines | Jesus Christ—History of doctrines | Jesus Christ—Person and offices | Salvation—Christianity | Jesus Christ—Miracles | Sanctification | Second Advent

Classification: BX6700.Z8 P142 2016 (print) | BX6700.Z8 (ebook)

Manufactured in the U.S.A.   09/29/16

To my mentors in the Fourfold Gospel,
some who are with Jesus:

my childhood pastor, Richard Harvey,
my first District Superintendent, Keith Bailey,
my Regina pastor, Richard Sipley,
and my colleague and often mentor, Al Runge.

—Franklin Pyles

To the Alliance Church congregations that
formed, nurtured, and sustain me:

Beverly Alliance Church (Edmonton, Alberta), my first
church, and the congregation led by pastor John Bell who first
introduced me to the vibrant life of Alliance spirituality;

Immanuel Alliance Church (Peterborough, Ontario) and
Cobourg Alliance Church (Cobourg, Ontario), who I had the
privilege to serve pastorally and who helped me learn the ways
of the deeper life through the joys and challenges of ministry;

Ancaster Village Church (Ancaster, Ontario), my current church
family who encourages and sustains me in the life of faith.

—Lee Beach

Contents

Preface

A GOOD IDEA DOES not necessarily stay a good idea forever. Ideas that inform, inspire, and empower can be of use for a time, but if they are not revised or updated, they can eventually become irrelevant. Good ideas tend to have a definite lifecycle. They initiate small, generating excitement and transformation among those who first hear and discuss the idea, so that they are catalyzed to disseminate it more broadly for others to also get excited about it and experience the transforming power of the new idea. Soon it has gained widespread interest, and perhaps, a movement has even been created. As with almost all movements, it takes on a life of its own, and while it still may embody the original idea, it also begins to move in ways that are independent of the original idea upon which it was founded. If the movement (which may have morphed into a full-fledged organization by now) is healthy, it will be able to sustain itself for a certain amount of time and continue to offer the transformative power of the original idea to those who continue to be captured by it. Eventually though, in the vast majority of cases, movements lose their momentum, and good ideas either have to be expressed in new ways or have to be resigned to the category of a former good idea that had its day but is no longer of use.

The fourfold gospel is a good idea. It captures things that are true about the message of Jesus Christ and that are essential to the understanding and practice of the Christian faith. For well over a century, the Christian and Missionary Alliance (C&MA) has been the movement that has carried this idea to the world. As a movement, the Alliance has grown and developed by being guided by the ideas that founded it: Jesus as savior, sanctifier, healer, and coming king. Its mission has been to preach the whole gospel to the whole world in a way that invites people to recognize Jesus as their savior and Lord, as well as the one in whom we find all of God's fullness for every aspect of our lives. The fact that A. B. Simpson, the founder of the Christian and Missionary Alliance, formulated a way of articulating this message that has resonated with millions of people throughout the years is a testimony to the simple brilliance of Simpson's conceptualization of the gospel message.

However, we live in an ever changing world and, as already noted, good ideas are not guaranteed to last forever. They need to be recast in new contexts and rearticulated in fresh ways, so that new life can be injected into them, in order that they become compelling to new generations of people.

And, these ideas need to be practiced. The Alliance must practice its belief that Jesus Christ is our savior, healer, sanctifier, and our coming king, and it must also understand why it believes that Christ alone is the way to God, the savior of the world, and why all of these truths compel us to preach and teach Christ everywhere. We have a sense that such practice is waning in Alliance churches, and that elders and laypeople, and perhaps even some pastors, do not fully understand the richness of these teachings and how they should be lived out. We hope to at least help people in our churches to begin again a journey of receiving and giving the benefits and blessings of Christ in the wholistic way that the Alliance has sought to present them.

Hence, this book, which came out of a conversation around the need for a fresh resource for Alliance churches, seeks to offer an engagement with Alliance distinctives with a view to providing some reflection on those distinctives in contemporary theological terms, as well as casting a vision for the spiritual possibilities that are resident in the Alliance's message. Alliance distinctives have always been more about spirituality than about theology. Dr. Simpson was a pastor, evangelist, and spiritual seeker, whose greatest desire was to offer a way into a full experience of Christ himself. The goal of this book is to present the distinctives of the C&MA in a similar way. While it is our hope that the book will help readers understand the message of the Alliance in fresh ways, ultimately, we hope that we will contribute to the cultivation of an "Alliance spirituality" that is centered in a relationship with Jesus Christ and his mission in this world. We present six key ideas in Alliance belief and practice—the four tenets of the fourfold gospel, as well as the concepts of "Jesus Only" and "Mission."

"Jesus Only" has been a central concept in Alliance spirituality since the inception of the movement. Dr. Simpson wrote a famous hymn with that title that reflects his belief that all of God's blessings for the spiritual and physical life are found in Jesus alone. The emphasis on Jesus is found in all of the doctrines of the fourfold gospel. However, it is also true that, in the current context of western culture, the idea that Jesus *only* is the way to experience God's fullness is controversial. It was probably controversial in Dr. Simpson's day too, but not in the same way as it is in the post-Christian West. Because of this cultural reality, we thought that it would be useful to explore this aspect of Alliance thought as a distinct chapter.

"Mission," while not officially a part of the fourfold gospel, is surely as much at the heart of the Alliance movement as any of the four doctrines in the fourfold formulation. We could not imagine writing a book on Alliance thought without a chapter on this topic.

There has not been a lot of resources produced for the Christian and Missionary Alliance in recent years that are specifically intended for use in the local church. Certainly, there are a number of useful academic volumes that have been written. Dr. Samual Stoesz's book, *Understanding My Church: A Profile of the Christian and Missionary Alliance*, published in 1968 and revised in 1988, offers an accessible and thorough overview of the Alliance movement, but we believe that the volume we offer here is unlike any other resource available today. While we hope that this book can be of value to the individual reader who wants to understand Alliance theology and practice, the book is also designed to function as a training resource for Alliance church leaders, ordination candidates, and elders' boards, and as a small group resource to help Alliance people of all backgrounds understand the dynamic message of the Christian and Missionary Alliance in the world today. As you will see when you begin reading the opening chapter, we have created a back story for the book that is an attempt to bring the contents of the book into conversation with the lived experience of its readers. Each chapter is also formulated as a sermon, so as to give it a sense that it is a work of practical theology and not just of abstract thought. Further, a discussion forum is provided that offers some interaction with the sermon and provides some further exploration of ideas that are presented in the sermon. Finally, a discussion guide is included so that the book can function as a resource for groups who want to discuss and digest these ideas in their own context.

With these things in mind, we want to acknowledge that the perspective of this book is decidedly North American, and in certain ways, is an attempt at expressing the main tenets of Alliance ideology in that context. We are in a time of tremendous transition in the Western church today, and as the opening example demonstrated, unless good ideas find fresh articulation in new contexts, they run the risk of becoming obsolete. We want to contribute something to the challenge that the contemporary church in the West is facing in expressing its faith in today's context. This does not mean that what is written here has no value to the Alliance church in other parts of the world, where in some cases, it is even stronger than it is in North America. Many of the ideas explored in this book are essential aspects of a robust Christian spirituality in any culture, and so we humbly offer our insights to believers in any culture where the message of the Christian and Missionary Alliance may be of relevance.

In closing, we would like to acknowledge that in preparing the manuscript for this book, we have received help from a number of sources. First, because we wanted to write a book that would actually be helpful to the Alliance constituency, we conducted a series of interviews with Alliance pastors, asking them what they thought the issues that needed to be addressed were and what kind of a book would be most useful. The responses that we received were tremendously helpful, and the input that was given has proved to be invaluable to us in our writing. Our thanks go out to the men and women who participated in that aspect of our research. We also want to thank Aaron Gerrard, Tommy Tsui, and Matt Kinniburgh for reading the manuscript and offering feedback and questions for us to consider in the development of the final draft and the discussion forums. Also, we want to express our thanks to our partners at MDC press, Dr. Stanley Porter and Dr. Hughson Ong for their support and help with this project.

The message that the Christian and Missionary Alliance embodies as a movement is a good idea. It is the good news of the gospel of Jesus Christ presented in a distinct way, for the sake of the world. We hope that this book can contribute to its ongoing renewal in our day and in the days to come. It is our hope that as you engage with it, you will be encouraged to press even more deeply into the fullness of Christ that the message of the gospel truly offers to all of us.

Franklin Pyles

Lee Beach

Back Story

IT HAD BEEN A number of years since I began my association with the Alliance Church. I was an undergrad student at a nearby university, and I practically stumbled on the church while working on a sociology project. The particular assignment that I was given in my Sociology 101 course tasked me with finding a group of people who were trying to make a difference in their community. I was supposed to investigate what they were doing and what motivated them to engage their community in this way. As it turned out, the bus that I took from the frat house that I lived in to the university went right past a local Alliance church. I had noticed a sign out front that advertized an "English as a second language" course that the church was holding. This seemed like something that fit the parameters of the assignment that I had been given, and so I decided to investigate it.

I come from a family that has a nominal Christian background, and I was not particularly interested in pursuing a deeper faith at that point in my life. However, this changed as I began my project and became acquainted with a number of the church members. My interest in Christianity was aroused as I talked to the various people whose lives had been touched by God through the church and who were now deeply involved in serving others through the various ministries that the church offered. In one way or another, I learned that my story is similar to the stories of many people who have not started out actually searching for God, but gradually became aware of his presence. It is kind of like the way we gradually become aware of the sun if we start out driving early

THE WHOLE GOSPEL FOR THE WHOLE WORLD

in the morning on a winter day. Slowly the light comes, and then the sun shows itself. It was like that with me, I thought I was researching the church and its people, but gradually, I became aware of another presence, God. He was, so to speak, researching me, simultaneously showing me to myself, and himself to me. I became a Christian, was baptized shortly after, married a wonderful woman who I met through a Christian campus ministry at the University I attended and, to my surprise, found a job in the same city. The Alliance church that I originally connected with is still my church home.

One Sunday, not long ago after the morning service, I was coming up the stairs from the nursery with our nine-month old daughter when Marge, one of the first people I met when I first made contact with the church and a great leader in our congregation, was heading down the stairs. Marge stopped me on the stairs and asked if she could talk to me for a moment. "Sure," I replied. I was definitely curious about what Marge wanted to see me about as we stepped into an empty room. Marge got right to the point, "As you know we are currently in the process of nominating elders for the congregation to consider at the annual meeting next month. As a member of the nominating committee, I have been asked to see if you would be willing to allow your name to stand to be an elder. What do you think, is this something you be willing to consider?" she asked with a smile.

As I took in Marge's words, I was at once pleased and at the same time dismayed. What would this mean? Was I ready for such a responsibility? We stood in silence for what seemed like minutes, but it was surely only a few seconds, as I found myself at a loss for words. I was glad to hear Marge's voice through the sudden fog that was filling my brain, "I'm sure that you will want to talk to your wife and pray about this for a few days. How about if I get back to you?" Marge said. "Yes," I stammered; "that would be great, I will consider it. Thanks." With that, Marge thanked me, grabbed my arm, and said, "I hope that you will really consider it. I think that you would do a great job. I'll pray that God will guide you." Marge gave me a wink as she left the room, leaving me with a mixture of excitement and trepidation and a decision to make.

My wife, Shelly, is always practical, and that frequently allows her to sense the issues that are really at play in a given situation. My wife reminded me that accepting this responsibility would take time, and she pressed me to consider if I was sure that I was ready to fulfill those duties. I thought that I could handle the time part, mainly because I saw this as an important thing to do, perhaps even as a calling that God was placing on me. I was also sure that I could, for the terms indicated, set aside some other things that I did not think were as important. But the question of "readiness" rattled me somewhat.

Shelly and I really prayed about it; we prayed very seriously over a period of several days. The longer we prayed, the more I had what can only be described as a sense of leading, or perhaps even calling, that I should allow my name to stand, even though I knew that this would definitely be a step into unknown territory.

When Marge approached me the following Sunday to ask me about my decision, I told her that I was willing to allow my name to stand and go through the nomination and election process. Marge was very kind and affirming when I announced this to her. She even hugged me and reminisced about the day we had met in the foyer of the church when I tentatively stepped in to begin my sociology project. Marge had been so welcoming to me when I was so far from being anyone who was ready to be an elder of a church, and now here I was accepting the nominating committees invitation to serve in that role. At the churches annual meeting four weeks later, I was elected to the board, and the congregation prayed for me and the other folks who were elected. They prayed that God would help us lead them and give us the strength to become an example to the congregation. I went home that night hopeful that I would be able to live up to those expectations.

Soon I found myself in one of the rooms in our church basement attending my first elders board meeting. The newly elected group of elders sat around two folding tables with bone white mugs of church coffee and the meeting agendas laid out in front of us.

The pastor welcomed us and reiterated the role of an elder in our congregation and the purposes of the board. After spending several minutes in prayer, we got down to business. I voted to accept the agenda and the minutes of the last meeting, we all listened to the reports and asked some basic questions about each one of them, and we also received encouraging words from the pastor about the overall direction of the church and its future plans. So far nothing was scary, and so I began to relax as the meeting progressed.

Towards the end of the meeting the chairman reminded us that the following Sunday was communion and that after serving communion we as elders should be prepared to pray for anyone who will come forward to ask for prayer for healing. This was a part of our church life that I had observed many times. However, now that I would actually be responsible to participate in this ministry, my mind started racing. I knew that our church believed in healing, and I affirmed that belief. After all, God is God, and he can heal anyone if he wishes. But, what was I supposed to do? What if questions were asked? Did I have the right kind of faith for this kind of praying? And, worst of all, what happens if we pray for someone to be healed and they aren't healed? Clearly, I had not thought about all of the responsibilities that were involved in accepting this kind of leadership role. Suddenly, I became aware that more was involved in being an elder than attending meetings and helping to form policy for the church.

That should have been enough for the evening, but next I was asked to put the "new member" class into my calendar and to be ready to interview those who finished the class and wanted to become members. Class? Interviews? What was I supposed to ask them, and what if they had questions about the church and the Christian and Missionary Alliance? I had been around long enough that I had some idea about these things, but now I was wondering if I was really able to answer any kind of significant question? Did I really know enough about our church and the movement that it was a part of? Suddenly, I was feeling unsure about my knowledge and experience as a person who claimed an Alliance church as their spiritual family.

These responsibilities were inspiring what seemed like a bit of near panic as I realized that there was a whole side of being an elder that was way beyond the routines of board administration. I had joined the spiritual leadership of an Alliance church, and now questions flooded my mind. What does our church really believe? What if I were asked a question, inside or outside of the class? And how could I significantly help the pastor in giving real spiritual leadership to the church? Where should I start?

Not knowing what else to do, I began some reading on my own. I had heard a lot about the founder of the Christian and Missionary Alliance, Dr. A. B. Simpson. I discovered some of his books located on the lower shelf of our church library, so I checked them out and began to read. My reading of Simpson can be described as sometimes beautiful and sometimes difficult. There were moments when Simpson's writing drew me to God and inspired me to seek him more passionately. Then there were other times when reading him left me confused and wondering what he was really trying to say. In the end, this strategy of self-education had mixed results. I definitely learned a lot, but I also found myself unclear about what the Christian and Missionary Alliance really stands for and what it means for us today.

While Simpson's writings did help me some, I needed more clarity. So on a chilly, rainy Spring afternoon, the trees still bear and the wind gently blowing across the parking lot, I made my way to the church and into the office of our lead pastor, Pastor Andrew.

"I want to be a fully functioning elder," I said, "I don't want to make stupid mistakes; I want to represent our church, serve it, support it, and support you. But, there is a lot that I don't get. For instance, the fourfold gospel thing, I know that it is an important part of who we are, but how does it work? What practical difference does it make? Why only four and no more? And healing, I know that God can heal, but I don't understand why he doesn't heal all the time and how my prayers as an elder work? Also, I don't want to make mistakes when I pray for people. Can you help me understand these things? I could really use some help in understanding what it is that we really believe as an Alliance family and how I can serve my church as a leader.

Pastor Andrew listened as I talked. He seemed genuinely interested in my thoughts, and I could tell that he took my concerns seriously. After over a half-hour of listening and discussion, he told me that he would like to think about my call for help and consider what might be the best way to address them. A few days later, my cell phone rang and he asked me to consider a proposal that he had developed. He told me that, as he thought and prayed about our discussion, he realized that the questions I was asking were not just questions that an elder needed to wrestle with but that they were questions for the whole church. Thus, he had an idea that he wanted my feedback on; he would preach a series of sermons on the core beliefs of the Alliance, including the fourfold gospel. Further, he would encourage people to email him questions about the sermon through the church website, and he would respond to those questions in order to clarify or further explain the foundational beliefs that form the essence of what it means to be "Alliance." In this way, he hoped to be able to attach the teaching to real questions. In addition, our associate pastor, Pastor Elaine, would prepare a special seminar for the elders on healing.

As pastor Andrew pointed out to me, the core beliefs of the Alliance go beyond what is commonly known as "the fourfold gospel." The Alliance believes that the gospel must be preached to the whole world and that it is good news because belief in Jesus opens the door to both eternal life and the renewing presence of Christ in the lives of individuals and the world around us. For this reason, the Alliance is a missionary movement, a group of churches that seeks to reach out with Christ's love in its local community but also sends people out to show Christ's love and to tell his story. I told Pastor Andrew that for sure I needed to know more about that. But even though I understood that this was a central belief of the Alliance, I also realized that I had some questions about it as well, questions like, "is Jesus the only way to God" and "what about people who have never heard about Jesus"? Pastor Andrew paused, and then chuckled as he answered, "this project is getting really big really fast," but we agreed that those questions could not be ignored.

From there, more questions tumbled out. Is "Jesus our Coming King" at all relevant to our day? And if we pray for healing and a person is not healed, does that mean we didn't have enough faith? Or does it mean that God doesn't heal? Sanctification? What is that? Is there an implication there that I can live without sinning?

As we talked, it seemed that the pastor's eyes just grew wider and wider, and I realized he must be saying to himself "what have I gotten myself into"? But, the truth of the matter is that highly involved laypeople and leaders in Alliance churches need to know and understand these teachings because they form the foundation of how we act and behave as a body of Christ. While they are crucial to Alliance spirituality, they are also key truths in the Christian life no matter what denominational movement you may be a part of. So, after more discussion and consultation, Pastor Andrew preached the sermons and answered questions about each one of them from various members of the congregation. The sermons and a sampling of the questions are presented to you here, not as the final word, but as a way for you, and perhaps your church, to begin your own discussion on these important ideas that shape and form the family of churches known as the Christian and Missionary Alliance.

1

Jesus Our Savior

INTRODUCTION

THERE IS A BOOK that was published several years ago called *The Day America Told the Truth*. In that book, the authors, James Patterson and Peter Kim, did a massive survey of the then current state of American morality. Among the questions they asked was, "What would you be willing to do for ten million dollars?"[1] Their findings revealed that twenty-five percent of the people surveyed said they would be willing to abandon all their friends. Twenty-three percent said they would be willing to work as a prostitute for a week. Sixteen percent would give up their citizenship. Ten percent said they would withhold testimony that would allow a murderer to go free. Seven percent would murder a stranger; so if there are approximately three hundred of us here today, look around because more than twenty people here could have you in their sights! Six percent would change their race, and four percent would have a sex-change operation.

These responses remind us that people are capable of doing anything and that the old adage "everyone has their price" is truer than we may like to believe. At the very least, questions like the ones I've highlighted here cause us to reflect on what it would take for us to compromise our integrity. They cause us to wrestle with who we truly are deep inside.

---

1. See Patterson and Kim, *The Day America Told the Truth.*

Our world is full of things that remind us of what human beings are capable of. Month by month, we are told of even more shocking events, such as mass shootings, abductions and forcible confinement, abuse of children, not to mention the harm done to us all through various kinds of financial fraud. Things like these bring to the forefront of our minds the reality of the depth of human depravity.

True, on one hand, we can easily keep these things at arm's length. None of us, at least I hope it is accurate to say this, have committed such heinous acts against another human being. Even the findings of Patterson and Kim might not necessarily connect with us personally. But if we are honest, and if we take a deep look into our own lives, we can see ways in which our own behavior and attitudes can reflect things that are very wrong. We may find ourselves in a broken relationship of one kind or another, and while the situation is most likely complex, if we are honest, we would have to admit that we have not always acted properly, and the brokenness of the relationship is at least in part the result of our poor behavior. We struggle with addictions and indulgences that we are not proud of and that we know are destructive to ourselves and maybe others. We have secrets that we keep, because we know that if they came out, we would be ashamed of things we have said, done, or thought.

I don't raise any of this in order to inspire guilt in anyone; we are all in the same boat when it comes to these things, and that is the point. We all live with a sense that life is not what it should be, and we are not all that we should be. This world is less than it is intended to be, and we are less than what we are intended to be. Both individually and corporately, we recognize that things are not quite right. As I said, most of us sense this keenly.

This morning we are embarking on a short journey through a number of affirmations that define the family of churches that this church is a part of—the Christian and Missionary Alliance. Over the next several weeks, we will look at how these affirmations are relevant to our lives and how they need to be understood so that their power and meaning can shape us as a church and as individuals. This morning we begin by affirming, "Jesus Our Savior."

Struggling with our own sin, surrounded by evil, we long for salvation, and our church proclaims, as a cornerstone teaching, every person can have salvation, for in response to the temptations, horrors, and struggles of our frail humanity, God offers us salvation through his son Jesus Christ. But why is this necessary, what does it mean, and how do we experience it? This is what I want to invite us to consider together this morning. Let's begin by considering why do we need a savior in the first place.

WHY THE NEED FOR A SAVIOR?

I remember reading a story about a hiker who was trekking along the path of the canyon of the Grand Teton Mountain in Wyoming. While walking across one of the canyon's hanging snowfields with a group of friends, he suddenly lost his footing and began to slide down the canyon wall. His friends watched him slide, expecting that he would eventually come to a stop so that he could be rescued, but he never stopped sliding. He slid further and further picking up speed as he descended until he disappeared out of the sight of his friends. His lifeless body was later discovered at the bottom of the canyon floor.

The hiker certainly did not start out expecting tragedy to strike; that was definitely not the intent of the expedition. All of us can tell a story like this about ourselves, a story of starting well but of taking wrong moral turns, of not paying attention to warnings, and of putting ourselves and the pleasure of the moment first and then experiencing dreadful consequences. How is it that all of us ended up in this story of dreadful consequences? To understand that, we must start at the very beginning when God created the world and then called it "good." This evaluation is offered six times in the creation story of Genesis 1. Then we read in Gen 1:27–28,

> So God created mankind in his own image,
> in the image of God he created them;
> male and female he created them.

God blessed them and said to them, "Be fruitful and
increase in number; fill the earth and subdue it. Rule
over the fish in the sea and the birds in the sky and over
every living creature that moves on the ground.

After the creation of humanity, God deems his creation to
be "very good." God has created a supremely good world, with
human beings as the ultimate expression of God's goodness. As
the Genesis story continues, more description is added. In 2:7, we
read that God formed the original human from the soil that he
had created. Out of the "good" stuff of creation, God forms Adam,
then in language that is powerfully dramatic, we are told that God
blew life's breath into the nostrils of the human, and the human
came to life. This is potent language because it offers a vision of
God's breath, that is, his very life being breathed into the human
so that he might live. This image is core to the biblical vision for
the intention of creation—God sharing his life with humanity. It
offers deeply relational connotations that draw our attention to the
intimacy that is intended between God and human beings. The in-
terchange between God and the original human demonstrates that
God has created us for deep relational familiarity. Further, we read
in 2:18 that there seemed to be one thing in creation that was yet to
be completed, and it was that he sees Adam alone, and God judges
it to be "not good." The relational nature of the man as rooted in his
relationship with God is unfulfilled without other human beings
to share life with. Thus, God creates woman as a partner for the
man. When presented with his partner, Adam declares,

This is now bone of my bones
and flesh of my flesh;
she shall be called "woman,"
for she was taken out of man.

Just as the original human being owes his life to the breath
of God, his life-friend/partner/co-regent owes her life to God's
creative actions and also to her human partner. The relational
closeness that this story depicts between God and humanity and

humanity itself is central to the ideal of creation as God intends it. This is the basic stuff of life, we are created by God for God, our lives are born out of his life giving intentions, and our lives are intertwined with one another's because God understands that human beings need relationship with other human beings.

But now, with all of this goodness, the disastrous wrong turn is made. Thus, we come to the next scene in the story that depicts the catastrophic severing of these relationships. As the scenario unfolds, the serpent whispers to Eve about the inadequacy of creation and tempts her and, ultimately, Adam, to reject the structure of creation as established by God and to set out on their own flight, thus rejecting God and establishing their autonomy apart from him. This is the essence of what is known as "the fall," and it is what is at the core of what we call "sin"—that is, that we are prone to reject God's creational intention for relationship with him and with each other. The result of the couple's decision to rebel against God reflects the consequences of this propensity. Immediately, we are told that they become aware of their nakedness. Prior to their deciding to eat the fruit from the tree that God had instructed them not to eat from, the couple apparently lived together in complete comfort in one another's presence. Nakedness depicts openness and ease between the couple; after the fruit is consumed, however, they immediately cover their nakedness because they are ashamed to be seen as they really are. Their ideal relationship has been disrupted by their choice to strive for self-sufficiency apart from God and each other. This captures part of the core of the human condition; we are afraid to be ourselves with one another. Of course, we are more comfortable with some than others, but at the core of human relationships is a striving for autonomy that makes us reticent to be in intimate relationship with those who we have been created to be in relationship with. The divine intention for relationship between people, in marriage and family, in community, and among the nations, was lost.

Furthermore, our relationship with God was deeply fractured. In Gen. 3:8, we read that, after the couple eats the fruit, God walks in the Garden, calling out for the couple, but they are fleeing from him, hiding in the Garden and hoping to not be discovered. The picture is one of God continuing to pursue relationship with his created beings; he wants to stroll with them in the coolness of the Garden, but the humans are now resistant to the pursuit. They have become afraid of God. The intimacy of creation is lost, and just as sin has brought disease to the human and to human relationship, it has also brought about a disease with God.

There is a legal aspect to sin, for it is breaking the law or missing the mark. To sin is to fall short. But, we must not think of "missing the mark" as "sometimes I hit it, other times I miss." No, the reality is much more serious than that. We are not even facing the target, let alone having the capability to hit it sometimes. Yes, good things can be done; we can love others or even worship God. But these are far from our natural inclinations. That is why we need a savior, we need one who will come and remind us of who God is, who we are, and who can rescue us from our resistant nature. We need one who can lead us back to the place where relationship with God begins again, and the possibility of relationship with one another is rekindled. And that place is the cross of Jesus.

A FULL SALVATION

This is a complete salvation, a salvation that makes us whole again, not focused on the minutia of individual sin, as terrible as that is. It is a salvation that is for each one of us and that brings about a future restoration of creation that is truly holistic.

Salvation does have individualistic dimensions to it and is directed to each of us, because God longs to have a relationship with every person he has created, but salvation also does encompass everything God has created, ultimately including the restoration of creation, a restoration that will include us, as we are raised from the dead just as Christ was raised from the dead (Rom 8:19–23). God saves us so that we can experience intimacy with him, just as he originally intended; he saves us so that we can participate in authentic relationship with others, and he saves us so that the whole of creation can be restored to its original intention, as a place of peace, harmony, and intimacy.

Why is Jesus central to this salvation story? In Heb 1:1–3, we read,

> In the past God spoke to our ancestors through the prophets at many times and in various ways, but in these last days he has spoken to us by his Son, whom he appointed heir of all things, and through whom also he made the universe. The Son is the radiance of God's glory and the exact representation of his being, sustaining all things by his powerful word. After he had provided purification for sins, he sat down at the right hand of the Majesty in heaven.

Jesus is the clearest revelation of God, and his ultimate purpose was to be the one who would bring repair to the broken relationship between God and human beings. Jesus' death and resurrection are central to this initiative, for Jesus' death on the cross is clearly depicted by the biblical writers as atonement for sin. This means that his death and the blood he shed cover the consequences of sin, provide forgiveness for sin, and offer the opportunity for a fresh start. His resurrection provides the path to new life and future hope. Jesus himself offers the ultimate goal of salvation in his prayer recorded in John 17. In John 17:20–21, Jesus prays to God the father using these words,

> My prayer is not for them alone. I pray also for those who will believe in me through their message, that all of them may be one, Father, just as you are in me and I in you. May they also be in us so that the world may believe that you have sent me.

Jesus' words demonstrate that the intention of God is that his disciples will enter into the divine life embodied in the Trinitarian nature of God. While we don't have time to explore the mystery of the Trinity, it is a core Christian belief that God exists as one being in three distinct persons: Father, Son, and Spirit. In this prayer, Jesus affirms his intimacy and oneness with the Father and prays that his followers would also share in this experience of intimate

oneness with both the Godhead and with each other. Jesus is praying a prayer reflective of the relational life that we are created for;
a life of intimacy, authenticity, and love with both God and our
fellow human beings. This is what Jesus came to bring; his death
on the cross and his resurrection offer us the possibility of restoration to God's original intention. The author of 2 Peter puts it
this way, "he has given us his very great and precious promises, so
that through them you may participate in the divine nature" (1:4).
Jesus comes to lead us back to the relational intentions of God as
depicted in the creation story of Genesis.

Jesus did not die to simply provide us with a ticket to heaven
(or the proverbial get out of jail free card). He came to offer us
abundant life by providing forgiveness for sin as the doorway into
intimacy with the Trinitarian life of God and, by extension, God's
family on earth, his church. This is the abundant life that Jesus
talked about in John 10:10, when he made clear that he came so
that we may have life and have it in its fullness. It is a salvation that
is wide in its scope, including not only the forgiveness of sin and
freedom from guilt, but also the participation by the Holy Spirit
in the divine life of God and reconnection with his created order.

In these days of the early twenty-first century here in North
America, this is a message that we deeply need to hear. This is the
message that the church has to offer to our society: the message of
Jesus' death as primarily a sacrifice for sin is less and less attractive
to a population who by and large does not understand, let alone
live by the categories that we as Christians use to define sin. As the
population is increasingly less shaped by the Christian message,
they no longer sense the need for a savior who offers them forgiveness for things they don't even feel bad about. This is not to deny
that all people are sinful and in need God's forgiveness. Rather, it
is to acknowledge that people no longer understand the world in
those terms. Thankfully, our gospel is about more than just juridi-
cal categories of guilt and innocence. It is about restoration of the
world. It is a good news message of renewed relationship between
creation and creator and between human beings. It goes to the essence of the human condition, that is, estrangement from God and

from one another, and offers the hope of repair and redemption. This is a message that is needed at all times and has special resonance in and for a time like ours.

EXPERIENCING SALVATION

Finally, we must consider how we can appropriate this message. Salvation has been likened to a gift that God has given, and we are thus invited to receive it. It is God's intention that each one of us receives this salvation, because it is in the recognition of our brokenness and need for Christ's work on our behalf that unlocks the potential for his salvation to work itself out in our lives. So our knowledge of the message of Jesus as our savior demands a response, a response of faith and surrender.

The apostle Paul makes it clear in Rom 10:9–10 that,

> If you declare with your mouth, "Jesus is Lord," and believe in your heart that God raised him from the dead, you will be saved. For it is with your heart that you believe and are justified, and it is with your mouth that you profess your faith and are saved.

Jesus put it another way,

> Then he said to them all: "Whoever wants to be my disciple must deny themselves and take up their cross daily and follow me. For whoever wants to save their life will lose it, but whoever loses their life for me will save it. (Luke 9:23)

Salvation is intended to change us and lead us into a new life that increasingly experiences a deepening relationship with God and a transformed relationship with others and the whole of creation.

What does this mean for us in tangible terms? First, it means that we have to take an honest look at ourselves and see that everything is not "alright" in us. There is the need to confront the bad news of sin, before we can experience the good news of redemption. In many ways, this is not in tune with much contemporary wisdom that advises us to focus on the positive voices and not to let negative thoughts take hold of us in the forming of our self-perception. However, there is a need in each one of us to come to honest terms with our own estrangement from God and the consequences that it has brought into our lives and relationship with others. Just like the cancer patient must come to terms with the diagnosis of a malignant tumor in order to enter into treatment that will bring healing from it, so we must have the willingness to face our own rebellion toward God and his ways. We must be willing to confess that the consequences of our rebellion are that we have gone wrong and that we need forgiveness and healing. This is sometimes hard to do. It can get ugly, but it is the beginning of salvation as we confront our sin, brokenness, and perhaps even our anger with God, others, and ourselves. But when we do this, it is the beginning of our coming to terms with our need for God's forgiveness and his help in giving us a new start.

Second, we surrender ourselves to Jesus in faith and commitment to his purposes by sincerely dying to ourselves and choosing to live for him. In doing this, we are saying that we believe that his ways are right, and that with the help of his spirit that takes up residence within us as we enter into the family and life of the Trinitarian God, we can enter into the process of transformation that God wants to enact in our lives. When we have done this, as Paul says, through believing in our hearts and confessing with our mouths that Jesus truly is Lord, the world opens up to us in dramatically new ways. God's healing power can be released into our life to "save" us from the pain, hurt, and guilt of our past. Broken relationships have new potential to be healed, things done and things left undone can be redeemed as we obey Christ's ways and move in his power. We can join in what God is doing in this world to bring the message of hope and redemption to all people.

God's salvation includes all of these things and more. When we take Jesus as our savior, we are fully entering into God's unfolding story and we become conscious participants in it. This changes everything about us as God's new life begins to work itself out within us.

CONCLUSION

This is salvation. The Christian and Missionary Alliance grew out of a message that emphasized a holistic gospel that offers a holistic salvation—a gospel that promised spiritual redemption, healing for the body, deep fellowship with God, and hope in this world and in the one to come. This is what we are invited to experience in the salvation that God offers, and this is what we mean when we declare "Jesus, our savior."

DISCUSSION FORUM

On-Line Interaction on the Sermon: "Jesus Our Savior"

Hi Andrew,

Thanks for the sermon on Sunday. There was a lot there for me (and everyone else) to think about, and it was a great challenge. One question that I have is how does the idea of good works fit into salvation? What is the difference between "doing good deeds" and "earning our salvation"? Thanks again for the message.

Paul

Paul,

Thanks for this question. It is one that many people wrestle with. Ephesians 2:10 says, " For we are God's handiwork, created in Christ Jesus to do good works, which God prepared in advance for us to do." We are created to do good works and are therefore expected to do them. If I ask my son to wash the car, and he washes it, I am grateful for his obedience, but he has not gained special merit from me by obeying me. But some believe otherwise. They see God as having placed us in what might be described as a neutral position where we can do things that are good or evil—if good, a reward comes, if evil, then a punishment is expected. Thus, if in the end a person is rewarded with heaven, it is because they choose to perform more righteous works than evil. This is not the vision of God or the gospel that we take, for if it were the case, we would be the ones who take ourselves to heaven as a result of our good works. No good work overcomes or outweighs sin, so we cannot save ourselves. Only God, against whom we sinned, can save us, and this is what he has done by coming to us in Christ and taking our sin upon himself. This is all the work of God and not something we can ever merit by our own efforts.

I hope that this answers your question Paul. Thanks for taking the time to send it in.

Andrew

Pastor Andrew,

I appreciated your sermon on Sunday, although I did find myself struggling with some of it. At a certain point you talked about the "minutia of individual sin" as if sin was not the primary thing that Jesus came to deal with. Further, when you say that people today don't identify with sin, and so we should make the gospel more attractive by not talking about it, does that not miss the point of Jesus coming altogether? In your attempt to emphasize the whole gospel, could it be possible that you are underemphasizing the main component of the gospel message, the forgiveness of sins? Also, is it important to make the gospel "attractive"? Isn't the gospel supposed to be offensive?

Thank you for the opportunity to ask these questions, I look forward to your response.

Sharon

Sharon,

You have raised some important issues with this question, thanks for asking it. I certainly did not intend to underemphasize the seriousness of sin. As you point out, this is a key issue, and it is at the heart of what Jesus came to address. We need forgiveness from sin, and

Jesus' death and resurrection (and his life) provide for this directly. What I wanted to bring out though was the fact that, when we only see Jesus' work as the forgiveness of sin, we are missing out on many aspects of Jesus' ministry that are of great significance for us. As I said in the sermon, the work of Jesus is not only to bring forgiveness for sin but also to bring healing to human relationships and to restore the possibility for us, as human beings, to enter into the relationship with God that we are created for. In my experience, too often the gospel that we have preached has been very narrow in that it *only* emphasizes the forgiveness of sin. We need a more holistic message that offers all of what Jesus came to do. He came to provide forgiveness, to offer abundant life by reconnecting us with the triune God, to provide purpose by connecting us to God's mission of reconciliation with all of creation, and to restore the brokenness of human relationships and create the possibility for unity among people from those restored relationships. Without all of these ideas included, the gospel message is incomplete. Personal sin is a serious matter that each of us has to come to terms with (as I talked about in the sermon), but there is more to Jesus' saving work than that. It addresses the sin that is intrinsic to creation and human relationships too. When we preach this, we have a message that encompasses the fullness of Jesus' gospel and offers a broad hope to our friends and neighbors. It is not about making the gospel more attractive as much as trying to offer a message that starts at a place that may resonate with people without compromising the essential elements of our message. I don't think that preaching the gospel has to start with human sin. It seems to me that Jesus never, or very rarely began there. There are many truths that the gospel offers and we need not be bound by one particular one as the essential starting point, when it comes to sharing the gospel message with others. I think that people are interested in how to make their lives and the world a better place. Whether we agree with them on this is probably not the issue; this is the place where most of them need to start if the gospel is going to make sense to them. Again, I don't mean to diminish the seriousness of sin, but I do want to help the church understand that there are many aspects to the gospel beyond forgiveness of sin. Perhaps engaging people with the gospel can begin with a discussion around spirituality (relating to God) and/or purpose (what are we here for?). Thankfully, the gospel addresses both of these issues. Once our friends understand that Jesus came to help them connect with God and participate in his good purposes for the world, the issue of sin will naturally follow. It is not that we should neglect this issue, but it is that we have to realize it is not the only starting point when it comes to helping people understand Jesus and what he came to do for us.

Thanks again for your questions Sharon, I hope this helps clarify things a bit.

Andrew

Hey Andrew,

Could you tell me more about what you were talking about when you brought up that whole thing about the Trinity? I'd never heard that before. It sounded kind of cool but also a bit hard to understand. I think I like it, but some further thoughts would be helpful. Thanks!

Adam

Hi Adam,

Thanks for taking the time to email this question. What you are asking is indeed a bit deep, and I don't promise to be able to explain it fully, but here it goes. The essence of our problem as human beings is that we are relationally disconnected from God and from the intimate relationship he intends for us—that is, that we should be engaged with him in his true essence as Father, Son and Spirit. This is the intention of God in creation, and it is what Jesus comes to save us "to." We often talk about what Jesus came to save us "from," but he also came to save us "to" some things, especially "to" a restored relationship with the God who created us for himself. This means a mean-ingful interaction with God as Father, Son and Spirit. This is where the abundant life of Jesus is found as we engage in the relational nature of God and discover our true humanity in this relationship and its outworking in our relationship with others. This is where the gospel goes well beyond simply offering forgiveness for sin (as important and central as that is) and offers us a full resto-ration to our essential humanity as those created by God to know him and bear his image. In practice, this means that we should see ourselves as people who belong to a community of friendship and intimacy. This is rooted in our friendship with God, who is the original, divine community and is further expressed in our relationship with the church, which is intended to be an expression of the divine community, and then in our relationship with the world, which is the place that God loves, is present in, and wants to restore to himself. Each of these relation-ships is rooted in God as the starting point. When we are right with him as a result of Jesus Christ's work on our behalf, then we have the potential to be right in these other relationships too. This is the heart of the gospel of Jesus as our savior.

Adam, I don't know if this is making things clearer or more murky, but the message of Jesus as savior is ex-pressed in the idea that he comes to save us "from" sin and "to" a relationship with the divine Trinity that at-taches us to God, his people, and the world he has always been deeply engaged with. Thus, Jesus as savior restores us to God and his purposes in this world. In other words, he sets things right again and invites us not only to be set right ourselves but to participate in setting things right in this world too. This is the Alliance message of "Jesus Our Savior."

Thanks for an engaging question Adam, I hope this answer helps a bit!

Andrew

QUESTIONS FOR FURTHER CONSIDERATION
AND DISCUSSION: "JESUS OUR SAVIOR"

What are some ways that we see sin manifest itself in the world today? How does this affect human relationships, and in what ways does it leave the world in a state different from what God intends?

How does sin manifest itself in your life? What are some ways that you personally see sin affecting you?

How does salvation as being individual but also impacting all of creation resonate with you? How is it different than ways you have heard Jesus as savior taught in the past? What do you find most hopeful about the message of the gospel stated this way?

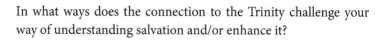

In what ways does the connection to the Trinity challenge your way of understanding salvation and/or enhance it?

How might this message connect with people in society today? What elements of it may be most relevant? Are there any ways it may offend or run counter-cultural?

Biblical texts to consider: Gen 1:26–28; Gen 3; Rom 8:19–23; John 17:19–20.

2

Jesus Only

INTRODUCTION

DESPITE OUR DIFFERENCES, IT was a friendly conversation. I was in youth ministry at the time, and the youth group that I was pastor of was involved in a car wash to help flood victims in Bangladesh. We were working hard to raise money for the unfortunate people in that developing country who had been devastated by torrential rains and overflowing rivers. Late in the afternoon, a man in his mid-thirties drove up in a pick-up truck, pulled into the car wash area, and jumped out of the vehicle with a big smile on his face, requesting that we wash his big black truck. He declared enthusiastically that he thought that what we were doing was admirable. He assured us that we were serving a great cause and that he was glad to help out with it. His enthusiasm was engaging, and I couldn't help but get caught up in a conversation with him as members of my youth group got busy spraying, soaping, and rinsing his half-ton.

Initially, our conversation focused on the need for people to help each other and on how encouraged he was to see a group of teenagers giving their time to help people half a world away who had been so badly stricken by natural disaster. He asked me if we were an organized group of some kind or were just a random group of people trying to make a difference. When I told him that we were a church youth group, he nodded his head and affirmed that faith in God was important in life. I agreed and asked him about his faith. My new friend then proceeded to tell me about his recent experience at a new age retreat center where he had spent several weeks focusing on his spirituality. He talked about how being spiritually centered was very important to him and told me that the time at the center had helped him achieve that goal. I listened with interest as he described some of his retreat experiences to me. As we talked further, I shared with him my own spiritual experience that centered on my relationship with Jesus Christ, and I asked him about his own relationship with Jesus. He was very clear that he appreciated Jesus and what he stood for, indicating to me that Jesus was one of his spiritual teachers. Here the conversation took a slight turn as I pressed him a little and shared my belief that Jesus is unique and that he is more than just one of many good spiritual teachers. But, in fact, he is the unique Son of God, the savior of the world and the one we are called to give our wholehearted devotion to. I could tell by his body language that my conversation partner did not agree with me, but nonetheless, he was very gracious; he affirmed my faith and told me that it was important for all of us to find our own spiritual path. I politely agreed but reiterated that I believed that, ultimately, God desired for us all to place Jesus at the center of our lives. Around that time, one of my young people approached us and told my friend that his truck was finished being washed. As we got up from the patch of grass we had been seated on, my friend smiled and handed me double the amount of money that we were charging for the car wash. He thanked me for the conversation, and as we shook hands, I also thanked him for the talk and for his kind donation. As he jumped into his truck and began to drive away, I realized once again how challenging it can be for people to accept the claim of Christianity that Jesus is not just one of the ways to God, but that he is the ultimate way for us to know and experience the fullness of God's redemption in our lives.

As we continue in our series on the things that our Christian and Missionary Alliance family of churches affirm as historic guiding beliefs, we come to this concept that is not officially one of the components of what we call the fourfold gospel, that is, Jesus as our savior, sanctifier, healer, and coming king. However, this component is still at the core of what we believe as a church movement; the idea that "Jesus only" is the one who provides us with salvation, sanctification, healing, and hope of the coming kingdom. We are taking time in our series to explore this aspect of our doctrinal affirmations, because it is central to the things that we dearly value as an Alliance family. The four beliefs affirmed in the fourfold gospel are centered in the person of Jesus Christ, and it is this centering reality of the person of Jesus that makes all the difference in our faith and the practice of that faith, because ultimately the fourfold gospel is not a series of doctrines to believe in, but it is rather a spirituality that is to be practiced. It is a way of life that is rooted in the person of Jesus and our ongoing relationship with him. As we begin to understand our Alliance heritage as a spirituality that centers us in Jesus rather than a series of doctrinal affirmations, it opens us to receive all that Christ has for us as a result of his life, death, and resurrection on our behalf. Let's explore this idea together.

THE UNIQUENESS OF JESUS

The founder of the Christian and Missionary Alliance, A. B. Simpson, was gripped by the idea that Jesus Christ was the one who could bring us into the fullness of a personal encounter with God. To know Christ is to know God, and this opens up the possibility of knowing the fullness of God. Simpson wrote a song called *Himself* that contains the simple chorus, "All in all forever, Jesus will I sing. Everything in Jesus and Jesus everything." This was an expression of his own experience and remains as a foundation of what I will humbly call Alliance spirituality—that Jesus is at the center of what God wants to do in our lives. One Alliance historian wrote, "It was Simpson's message that Jesus abiding in the believer's heart and life brings into reality all the deeper experiences and truth recorded in the Acts of the Apostles and the New Testament Epistles."[1] This is indeed what the concept of "Jesus only" offers us,

1. Stoesz, *Understanding Your Church*, 130.

that through relationship with Christ, we enter into the mystical reality of knowing God, and thus the possibility of experiencing his presence and power in our lives.

As the conversation with my friend at the car wash illustrates, this is not an easy concept for a pluralistic, multi-faith society to embrace. That Jesus is somehow greater than the Buddha or Mohammed is an unwelcome opinion in our day. That Jesus is the center of things does not sit well with people whose faith is akin to an off-the-shelf self-help program, designed to create a sense of well-being and self-esteem, a faith that believes that God exists and that he created the world and watches over it, that God wants people to be nice to each other and help their fellow humans as the Bible and most world religions teach their followers to do, and that God wants people to be happy. Such a faith offers a God that is not overly involved in people's lives, unless we have a problem and ask him for help, and that is serene in the belief that ultimately most people will go to heaven because they are basically good.[2] This is the faith of mainstream North American culture, and we make a mistake if we think that people are not committed to it.

People are committed to it. Our friends, neighbors, and family members who may not profess faith in a specific, established religion, but who have and are committed to a faith that is moralistic, promote inner healing with a God who is there sometimes to help but seldom to interfere. To offer the centrality of Jesus to them is to violate a core doctrine of their benign, all-inclusive belief in who God is and how he works in this world.

However, for Christians, Jesus is our center, and we believe that there is something in him that cannot be found anywhere else. This does not deny the idea that God is at work in this world in a multitude of ways, or that other faiths are of no value. While we affirm the centrality of Jesus in salvation, we also need to affirm that God works in many different ways to bring people to that realization. Yet, at its core, Christian belief asserts that, in order to experience the fullness of God, we must come to Jesus.

2. See Smith, *Souls in Transition*, 154-55.

There are at least three aspects of Jesus' uniqueness that are part of this core Christian belief that Jesus only is central to our relationship with God.

The Uniqueness of Jesus as God's Son

The Gospel of John is most explicit about this issue, for John gives us an elevated portrayal of Jesus as the divine Son of God. In the opening verses of the Gospel, John clearly offers his perspective that Jesus is absolutely unique as the God who has come in human form to dwell among human beings on earth. He writes in John 1:1–3, "In the beginning was the Word and the Word was with God and the Word was God. He was with God in the beginning, through him all things were made, without him nothing was made that has been made."

Then in John 1:14, John makes clear who he is referring to when he writes, "The word became flesh and made his dwelling among us. We have seen his glory the glory of the one and only Son who came from the Father full of grace and truth." In these verses, the gospel writer equates Jesus with and to God. In the mindset of ancient Jewish people who would have read this work, there was only one way to understand this idea, as scandalous as it may have seemed, that God became human.

Further, John makes clear that Jesus becomes the object of derision and violence because of his claim to be equal with God. In John chapter 8, Jesus gets into a conversation with some religious leaders about who he is, and he asserts his uniqueness by stating to the religious leaders that he is greater than one of their greatest patriarchs, Abraham. In fact, he tells them that he is older than Abraham, which draws a question about the veracity of such a claim. Jesus responds by saying, "Very truly I tell you, before Abraham was, I am." The text goes on to report that the religious leaders picked up stones to stone Jesus, but he slipped out of their grasp. Why did these leaders want to stone Jesus? Because by invoking the phrase "I am" to describe himself, he was identifying himself with the sacred name of God as it was revealed to Moses in

Exodus 3. This is a clear indication that Jesus understood himself as God in human flesh. A similar scenario is played out in John 10. Here Jesus is again claiming oneness with God, and we read again that the Jewish leaders picked up stones to stone Jesus, but Jesus says to them, "I have shown you many good works from the Father, for which of these do you stone me?" They reply, "We are not stoning you for any good work, but for blasphemy because you, a mere man, claim to be God" (John 10:31–33).

John offers to us the uniqueness of Jesus as God incarnate, which is a staggering claim to be made, and presents a genuine reversal of expectations, for it did not seem right that God himself would come to meet humans on their own terms. It is kind of like the Queen of England coming to your house and mowing your lawn. Can you imagine answering the door one Saturday morning, and there stands the queen in her sensible shoes, patent flower dress, purse over her wrist, and tiara positioned firmly on her grey head, announcing to you that she was going to mow your grass for you? Then before you could protest, she was at it, methodically going up and down your lawn carefully pushing the lawn mower so as to not miss a spot. There you are standing at your window looking out thinking to yourself that something is not right here. This is a complete reversal of the way things usually work. But this is what God did—he chose to show up in a place and in a way that was unexpected.

In John's Gospel, there is a clear and profound emphasis on Jesus' humanity and the material/corporeal reality of Jesus as a person. John is clearly committed to depicting the reversal of things in this world as God becomes man in the person of Jesus of Nazareth, but he is also committed to depicting Jesus as the God who is fully human. Thus, we see Jesus at a wedding in John 2, and later in the same chapter, we see him show his emotions as he goes into a tirade against the merchants in the temple courts, turning over tables and angrily driving the corrupt businessmen out of the sacred space. We see him thirsty and seeking a drink from a woman at a well in John 4. In chapter eleven, Jesus weeps. In John 13, he straps a towel around his waist and washes feet. As committed as John is to presenting the divine Jesus, he is equally committed to presenting the reality of Jesus' humanity.

In the ancient world, it was not uncommon to have stories of men who were thought to be gods. This kind of story can be found in ancient writings, and it is part of the lore and belief systems of ancient people. What is a wonder to the author of John is not that a man could be a god but that God could be a man. The incarnation offers a radically different idea than the perspective that it is possible for a human to somehow possess a divine nature. For John, the wonder is that the divine has become human. If we note John 10:33, we see that in the conversation between the Jewish leaders and Jesus, the problem for his opponents is that, as a man, Jesus is claiming to be God. His opponents have seen this before; Jesus is a man trying to elevate himself to the status of God, and it is their responsibility to respond to this kind of blasphemy by putting a stop to it. But John's Gospel tries to demonstrate that the opposite is true. Right from the outset of his Gospel, John is concerned with presenting the concept that God has become human. It is not a human adopting something of the divine nature, but it is God himself taking on human form. In lowering himself in this way, God's actions indicate that something is happening that changes everything.

When we speak about "Jesus Only," this is what we are talking about: as the God-man, Jesus Christ is the one in whom God's work finds its ultimate and most poignant expression—the power and ministry of God are manifest through him in a potent way. This leads us to the second aspect of Jesus' uniqueness.

The Uniqueness of Jesus as the Agent of God's Work

Jesus himself teaches that he is the unique agent of God's work on earth near the beginning of John's narrative. In John 1:43–51, we see Jesus interacting with a number of people who will eventually become a part of his group of twelve disciples. As the conversation unfolds, one of them, a man named Nathanael, declares, "Rabbi, you are the Son of God, you are the king of Israel" (John 1:49).

This is a confession of Jesus' uniqueness, for a first-century Jew like Nathanael to say such a thing was for him to recognize that Jesus was not one among many who did the work of God. Rather, he was one above all others, when it came to his standing as the unique agent of God's working. However, what Jesus says next is even more astonishing. John 1:51 tells us that Jesus responds to Nathanael's declaration with these words, "Very truly I tell you, you will see heaven open, and the angels of God ascending and descending on the Son of Man." This is a direct reference to the Old Testament story of Gen 28:10–19, where Jacob experiences a dream in which he saw a staircase with one end of it resting on earth and its top extending to heaven. On the staircase, angels were ascending and descending between the place where God dwells and the place where humans dwell. In his dream, God assures Jacob of the great plans that he has for him, and when he awakes, he is aware that the place where he has slept is a special place: "Surely the Lord is in this place, and I was not aware of it." He was afraid, and he said, "How awesome is this place! This is none other than the house of God; this is the gate of heaven" (vv. 16–17). Jacob set up a pillar as a marker and called the place Bethel, which means, "House of God."

When Jesus makes reference to this story, he equates himself with the place that Jacob called the "House of God, the gate of heaven." Jesus is saying that he is the place where God dwells and that in him is the manifestation of God's work, the gate of heaven, and all that that means in terms of God's coming to earth to do his work. In Jesus is the coming of God and the power of his presence. When we affirm "Jesus Only," we are affirming that fact. We are recognizing that in Christ are all the possibilities of God's work being made manifest in our lives and the life of his church. This is the foundation of the third perspective at the heart of our belief in "Jesus Only."

The Uniqueness of Jesus and Christian Spirituality

Just prior to Jesus' revelation of himself as the "ladder" to God, John 1 depicts two young men following after Jesus, because they have heard that he is someone special who may have a message from God. The text tells us in v. 38 that Jesus turns to these would-be disciples and asks them, "What are you looking for?" This is the central question that John's Gospel is concerned with, because it is the central question for human spirituality. Through the ages, the question, "What are you looking for?" is the question that drives spiritual pursuit in the lives of human beings. Thus, for those of us who have been and are being shaped by the Alliance concept of the fourfold gospel, we recognize that, at its core, the four elements of this doctrinal construct are not doctrines to be affirmed as much as they are spiritual truths to be experienced. Jesus as savior, sanctifier, healer, and coming king are not theological concepts that define correct belief, or function as a set of ideas that determine theological orthodoxy. They are aspects of the life-giving work of Jesus being played out in our day-to-day relationship with the living God. As we have considered, Jesus is central to this spiritual experience. It is in relationship with him that the salvation of God explodes into our souls and the realm of sanctification is opened to us, and so is the free flow of God's healing power in all its dimensions made available to us. Also, the hope that Christ will return to restore a broken, fallen creation, which includes us, becomes a living hope in our lives.

These doctrinal truths are a part of what we might call "orthodox" Christian beliefs, and we affirm them, but they maintain no transformational power in our lives apart from a personal encounter with Jesus. Only Jesus can unlock the relational power of God's presence in our lives, and that is why our belief in the fourfold gospel is only dead doctrine, unless we also hold the belief that Jesus alone can turn these affirmations into a living spiritual experience, which is what Simpson had in mind when he began espousing the potential of the fourfold gospel as a way for Christians to think about their spiritual walk with God. Thus, when he wrote the chorus of his famous hymn, *Jesus Only*, he wrote, "Jesus only, Jesus ever, Jesus all in all we sing, Saviour, Sanctifier, and Healer, Glorious Lord and Coming King." This is not a doctrinal affirmation, this is an invitation to enter into the divine life and experience God's fullness. It is a reflection on the possibilities of living in relationship with God through Jesus Christ. It is a spirituality that centers on Jesus and affirms that through him all the possibilities of knowing God's presence and power are ours. When we affirm the idea of "Jesus Only," we are embracing God's ultimate self manifestation in Christ as an essential element of entering into the fullness of life that God has made available through relationship with his one and only Son. This is the provision that he has made for us, and the invitation that we are given to know God in all of his living reality.

CONCLUSION

The conversation that I had with that young man at the car wash provided me with a point of clarity that I have never forgotten. He was a true spiritual seeker; of that I am sure. He was a good man with a sincere heart. I have no doubt about that. I enjoyed talking to him, and I think we could have easily become friends if our paths had intersected in more than simply a passing fashion. However, if I could have that conversation again, I would take a slightly different approach. That day at the car wash, I wanted to convince him of the doctrinal superiority of Jesus against his nebulous new-age spirituality that emphasized finding one's "center." While pointing him to Christ would still be my goal, contending for the centrality of "Jesus Only" as a doctrine that must be believed would be less important to me than inviting my friend to consider how Jesus manifests God's presence and invites us into the experience of knowing God intimately. This is the idea that is at the center of "Jesus Only," and it is where the potency of this truth ultimately lies.

Inviting belief in Jesus as the primary path to God will always mean going against the grain of contemporary ideology. That is why that conversation provided me with a reference point, one that brings me back to the question about the uniqueness of Jesus. Is he really central to God's ultimate intention for us? Is true spirituality rooted in his life and work among us? Does trusting him in faith truly release the potential of God's fullness into our lives? Our response to these questions as Alliance Christians is "yes." Jesus is the pivot of God's work in the world and the person in whom we find God's fullness.

In declaring "Jesus Only," we affirm that, ultimately, the work of God in our lives flows through Jesus, and it is in Jesus only that God is found most fully and most truly. This is the message that drives our movement as Alliance churches and offers us the possibility of a vibrant spiritual experience that we can in turn offer to the world.

DISCUSSION FORUM

On-Line Interaction on the Sermon: "Jesus Only"

Hi Pastor Andrew,

Thanks for your message on Sunday and for having this forum as a place to ask questions. I'm not sure yet on how to properly word this question, so please bear with me. The idea of "Jesus Only" is a deep challenge to the way most people think in our culture; to be honest, I was challenged by your message to consider my own view on this. I am not sure I really see the world that way, but I do understand that this is a major part of the Christian message, and I want to definitely give Jesus his rightful place in my life. How do you propose that I make a shift in worldview? A shift in worldview is an easy thing to decide to do, but is an incredibly difficult thing to actually do it. Do you have any thoughts on how I can get there in my thinking especially when the message I get from almost everywhere else is that this is wrong? I hope this makes sense. Thanks again.

Sabrina

Hi Sabrina,

Your question makes perfect sense, and it is a good one. I appreciate your honesty. I think that many of us struggle with this concept in various ways because it is so counter to our culture. Just like you said, it goes against almost every message we hear. It is perhaps helpful to remember that this idea was a challenge to the first-century people among whom Jesus himself and the early church lived. For them to believe in the centrality of Jesus was not easy either. Also, it is important to remember that, in embracing faith in the uniqueness of Jesus, you do not have to completely dismiss the validity of other faiths or worldviews. We don't understand "Jesus Only" to be a repudiation of everything else, it is rather a belief that, ultimately, he is the head of everything and that everything else must align itself under his lordship. This does not mean that nothing else matters or that nothing else is true, but that it must just be seen in the light of Christ's ultimate headship over all things. Colossians 1:18 says, "He is the head of the body, the church, who is the beginning, the one who is firstborn from among the dead so that he might occupy the first place in everything." It is this idea of "first place" that "Jesus Only" reflects.

In terms of shifting your worldview, I think that you may want to reflect further on some of the material I shared in the sermon from the Gospel of John. Jesus' divinity, and thus his lordship over all things, is an act of grace and humility as God comes to us to reveal himself and restore his relationship with us. It is not an act of power, but is rather an act of giving up power for the sake of humanity. This is the one whom we are invited to call "lord." This is the distinctiveness of Jesus—God humbling himself and entering into life with us. This is the genuine uniqueness of the story that we are called to enter into and that makes him worthy of our commitment. We have to come to a place where we believe that this historical act of God stands above all other ideas, and all other ideas must be understood (or even evaluated) in light of it. I hope that this response helps you a bit as you wrestle through this issue.

Andrew

Andrew,

I hope that you had a good day off yesterday; I had a question about your sermon on Sunday. As I thought about your conversation with your friend at the carwash, I couldn't help but wonder how difficult it would be for him to accept the message of "Jesus Only" for a number of reasons. How do I prove this to someone? Can it even be proved? And how do I respond to someone who says, "that's great for you, but it doesn't need to be true for me." Thanks for taking time to answer this Andrew.

Jason

Hey Jason,

Thanks for taking time to send me this question, it is a good one, and one I am sure many others will have after Sunday's message. I don't think that you can "prove" the exclusivity of Jesus. While there are certainly valid arguments to be made for it (which I won't go into here), to say we can "prove" it may be promising something more than we can deliver. Let's face it; ultimately, it is a step of faith. I think the best way to demonstrate its truth is for those of us who follow Jesus to live in a way that demonstrates the qualitative difference about what being in relationship with Jesus actually brings to our lives. Like I emphasized in the sermon, "Jesus Only" is more of a call to spirituality than to doctrine. It is about finding God in Jesus and pressing into him, so that we can be transformed through our knowledge and experience of God. As we grow in wisdom, in our love for others, and in our ability to share God's grace, and as our lives are healed from sin and brokenness, the uniqueness of Jesus is made manifest in a way that speaks more loudly than any well-crafted argument (although there can be a place for that too). When people say, "that's great for you, but not for me," I am not sure there is much we can do, except to continue to stay in relationship with them and to trust God to continue doing his work in both them and us. Thanks again for the question, Jason.

Andrew

Dear Pastor,

I have a question about your sermon on Sunday morning that I would like you to clarify for me. I am glad that you are taking the time to teach on Alliance doctrine, but I was a bit concerned when you expressed that you thought there was value in other faiths and that God works in the world in a variety of ways. What did you mean by that?

Dell

Thanks Dell,

Fair question. I did say that and kind of moved on without much clarification. What I meant was I think that God is always at work in the world, present with people, and active in their lives, even if they do not know or understand it through the Christian lens that you and I would use. I think that Scripture and experience teach us that God works in multiple and sometimes mysterious ways to accomplish his purposes, and when we talk about "Jesus Only," we are not saying that God is only working when Jesus' name is invoked. This speaks to the topic of other religions too. I think we can affirm that, when we explore other religions, we will find various teachings that are in harmony with what the Bible teaches. From that perspective, there is some "truth" to be found in other religions. Romans 2 teaches us that people everywhere know God's truth. As an example, the core teaching of hospitality, honoring parents, and not stealing is widespread in other faiths, even though there are clear disagreements about God, his nature, and salvation, although of course we do not want to minimize these. In Sunday's message, I was only meaning to clarify that, when we promote "Jesus Only," it does not mean that we dismiss all other religions as completely invalid. Hope that clarifies things a bit, thanks Dell.

Andrew

Hi Andrew,

Your sermon on Sunday was highly informative for me; I had never heard some of those things put quite that way before. Thanks for the message! However, your last point and conclusion was the most significant, but also, frustrating part. You emphasized experiencing Jesus and how that leads us into the fullness of God. How do I, as a dedicated Christian who wants to grow/mature in Jesus, move beyond believing this to be true to experiencing it as present reality? Thanks for any thoughts you have on this!

Christine

Hi Christine,

Thanks for this, and I appreciate you pressing me for further reflection on this, because it really was at the heart of the message on Sunday, and because I think it is at the heart of the idea represented by "Jesus Only." As I reflect on your question, I wish that I would have offered a bit more on this in the message, because I think that part of what this meant for the founder of the Alliance, A.B. Simpson, was that he would radically trust Jesus by stepping out in faith for things like healing, evangelism, and large ministry projects that would take miracles to see come to fruition. His belief that Jesus would meet him and others, if they just trusted him, was at the core of his trust in "Jesus Only." Perhaps this is how you need to move into a deeper experience in your own life? Learning to listen to and trust in the Spirit. Can Jesus guide us to people who need a word from him through us? Can he guide us to pray more frequently and more confidently in faith for the healing of others? Can he lead us into "divine appointments" with people who are seeking him but need someone to bear witness? I think that we often equate pressing into Jesus with doing things like praying more, reading the Bible more, going on retreats more, all of which are crucial to Christian spirituality. But I think that in order to experience the uniqueness of Jesus more fully in our lives, we need to be attentive to his Spirit's leading and to step out in faith to join him in what he wants to do in this world. It was in doing this that Simpson experienced healing, saw God work in power, and encountered God's miraculous provisions for his life and work. As I write this, I know that I also need to cultivate this in my own life, but I think it is one of the key ways forward for me, our church, and maybe you too, Christine, to experience the fullness of Jesus more deeply. It is an ongoing process for all of us (which we will think about on Sunday in the next sermon in the series!). Thanks again for taking the time to send me your question.

Andrew

QUESTIONS FOR FURTHER CONSIDERATION AND DISCUSSION: "JESUS ONLY"

Have you ever had an experience similar to the one at the beginning of the sermon where you have had a discussion with someone who is genuinely spiritual or religious but rejects the idea of the centrality of Jesus? Perhaps you have had a discussion about Jesus with someone who has little or no interest in spiritual things. Describe one or more of those encounters.

Do you think that the term "cultural faith" offered at the beginning of this chapter is a reasonably accurate description of the way a lot of people think today? Do you agree with the idea that they are "committed" to their "faith?"

How does the claim that Jesus is ultimately central to salvation and the spiritual life resonate with you personally? Are there ways that this creates tension in your own mind or experience?

How do the three ways that the sermon presents Jesus as unique resonate with your own understanding? Does it add to it in any way? Does it challenge it?

Which Biblical text referenced in the sermon do you find most helpful in contemplating the idea of Jesus' centrality to spiritual life?

How does the message of Jesus only challenge the beliefs of contemporary culture? How can the message of "Jesus only" be presented effectively in that context?

Biblical texts to consider: John 1:1–14, 35–51; 10:22–33; Acts 4:5–12; Col 1:15–23.

3

Jesus Our Sanctifier

INTRODUCTION

I REMEMBER MY WEDDING day well, even though it is now almost twenty-five years ago. While certain details have faded
with time, many of the moments from that day remain clear in
my mind. One thing I remember was something that the minister
who wedded us said in his sermon prior to our exchange of vows.
The minister was actually my father-in-law, and my recollection is
that his sermon was rather long, and truthfully, I do not actually
remember much of it, but at least one thing did stick; he reminded
both my bride and me that marriage was not so much about finding the right person as is was about being the right person. He
encouraged us to give ourselves fully over to one another and to
do our best to be the right husband and the right wife for one another. He assured us that, as we focused on being the right person
for one another, we would find that our marriage would thrive. In
the subsequent years, I have found this advice to be wonderfully
true. While I am far from the perfect husband, I have tried to live
according to my father-in-law's wisdom. My wife, who is perfect
(what else am I going to say?), has also sought to live her father's
wisdom out. Actually, it is a rather counter-intuitive idea. We don't
normally associate happiness and wholeness with giving ourselves
over to someone else. The idea of submitting to someone else is
usually something we would rather avoid, and yet that day, as I

stood at the altar, that was what I was called to do, with the promise that it was the best decision that I could ever make.

This principle is also foundational to our spiritual lives. As we continue to consider the ideas that have shaped the Christian and Missionary Alliance as a movement, we come to the second doctrine in what is known as our fourfold gospel, the concept of sanctification. Sanctification is a central concept to Alliance spirituality and also to the whole of the Christian life. To "sanctify" literally means to "make holy or set apart for holy purposes." This is why the marriage illustration relates to this doctrine. Just as a bride and groom are called to give themselves over to one another, our sanctification is connected to the idea of giving ourselves over to God—to be set apart for his purposes in our lives. Similar to marriage, it involves commitment, submission, and trust, with the belief that in giving ourselves over to another in this way, it will lead to a life of great blessing. As already mentioned, in many ways, this seems quite counter-intuitive in our contemporary world. However, as a movement that has over one hundred and twenty-five years of history behind it, the Christian and Missionary Alliance has made the call to sanctification one of its core ideas in the cultivation of a vibrant spiritual life.

SANCTIFICATION IS ROOTED IN RELATIONSHIP

Sanctification is rooted in relationship; that is, our sanctification is rooted in God's redeeming purposes and in our desire to know and follow Jesus. The idea of being set apart for holy purposes does not begin with us, but it begins with God and his desire for us to know him and experience him in a deep and meaningful way. Sanctification is part of God's redemptive purpose in the world and in our lives. His desire is that we would be people who come out of the world, away from the decaying and corrupt structures and practices that often typifies life in a fallen world and be set apart for God and his purposes. Thus, sanctification starts with God desiring to be in relationship with us, and his acting in our lives in order to draw us to himself.

Thus, it follows that God's sanctifying purposes start in our lives at our conversion. It begins when we turn to Jesus and surrender ourselves to his lordship as savior. In Romans 8, the apostle Paul makes this clear to his readers: "There is now no condemnation for those who are in Christ Jesus, because the law of the Spirit who gives life has set you free from the law of sin and death" (vv. 1–2). At the beginning point of our salvation, God, by his Spirit, sets us free or sets us apart from the sin that keeps us away from his intentions for us. His desire for us to be set apart for his purposes takes root as his Spirit takes up residence in us through the saving work of Christ.

While being set apart for holy purposes does not begin with us, it does include us in a very important way. We have to make the choice to yield or say "yes" to God's desire to sanctify us. Before I married my wife, I had a great desire to do so. I wanted to be in a deep, long-term relationship with her with all my heart, and so the day came when I asked her, "Will you marry me?" My desire was key to this question being asked, but a wedding would never happen unless my desire matched hers and she said "yes." So also the beginning of the sanctified life is rooted in relationship, because it takes two to make it happen. In order to be sanctified, we have to want to be sanctified. God desires it, he provides the way for it, and we respond with our "yes"; the result is that we are set apart by God and sanctified for his purposes. As we accept God's invitation to believe in him through Jesus Christ, our sanctification occurs, and we can continue the process of living out its reality. In Rom 8:10–11, Paul speaks about the reality of sanctification as it begins to take root in our lives: "But if Christ is in you, then even if your body is subject to death because of sin, the Spirit gives life because of righteousness. And if the Spirit of him who raised Jesus from the dead is living in you, he who raised Christ from the dead will also give life to your mortal bodies because of his Spirit who lives in you."

This is not the end of God's sanctifying work in us any more than the wedding is the end of the marriage. Sanctification begins at conversion, but it continues and grows deeper as we continue to desire more of God and sense a need for further transformation in our lives, so that our "set-apartness" begins to become more demonstrable in our everyday behavior. This brings us to recognize that sanctification is the process of learning to trust Christ.

SANCTIFICATION AS TRUSTING JESUS

Trust is at the heart of every relationship. When my children were young, we would play a little game where they would climb up the first three or four (maybe five!) steps on the staircase in our house, and then they would leap forward, flying into my arms, and I would catch them (I may have missed a few times). That little game was rooted in trust. My son and daughter believed they could throw themselves off the stairs, and their dad would catch them and see to it that they landed safely on the ground, but only to repeat the exercise for as long as dad was willing to stand there catching. Essentially, they trusted not only in my physical ability to catch them but also in my character as a father. They believed that I would not want them to get hurt, and so I would do whatever is necessary to make sure that the game proceeds safely. Our relationship was full of trust. All healthy relationships are founded and built on trust, frankly so are some unhealthy ones, without it a relationship cannot grow. Lack of trust will kill a relationship. Sanctification is part of the process of growing in our relationship with Jesus, and thus, it calls for us to trust that he is both willing and able to deal with us in a way that will lead us deeper into the fullness of God's purposes. The process of sanctification is highly relational and continues the kind of mutuality that it began with. God desires to give us more of himself, but he also desires for us to give him more of ourselves too. As he continues to initiate, we must continue to respond with a "yes." And like any relationship that is growing in intimacy, the ongoing work of sanctification in our lives is a matter of practicing trust.

Paul frames it this way in Rom 8:12–13: "Therefore, brothers and sisters, we have an obligation—but it is not to the sinful nature, to live according to it. For if you live according to the sinful nature, you will die; but if by the Spirit you put to death the mis-deeds of the body, you will live." Note how throughout Romans 8 Paul keeps speaking about the concept of "life"; he is interested in helping his readers experience the life that God can give to them. Clearly, it is not physical life that Paul has in mind; he knows as well as we do that you can live a life of sin and carry on living quite well. What he is talking about is a certain kind of life, the kind of life that God imparts when we turn to him in trust, so that his Spirit can enter into our life and transform our relationship with him, with others, and with the world. This is the sanctified life.

Paul emphasizes our part in experiencing this life in its full-ness; "we have an obligation" he says, and that obligation is to co-operate with God's working in us by "putting to death the misdeeds of the body." If we are going to experience the life God has for us, we are going to have to trust that his life is much better than what we can find elsewhere, and, as a result, we have to give ourselves to him and to the process of cultivating his life that is now in us. To go back to our marriage metaphor, it is just like the newly married couple who have chosen to forsake all others in order to give them-selves wholeheartedly to each other. Their "obligation" is to focus on their spouse and developing that relationship. The process of sanctification continues to develop in us as we respond to God's promptings to go deeper with him and submit to him, so that his transformative purposes can be worked out in and through us.

How does this happen? In the book of Ephesians, Paul also calls his readers to forsake their former ways and move forward into the life that God has called them to. He reminds them of the corrupted ways of the world and the futility of living that way, and then he uses this language to teach the process of sanctification to the church: "That, however, is not the way of life you learned when you heard about Christ and were taught in him in accor-dance with the truth that is in Jesus. You were taught, with regard to your former way of life, to put off your old self, which is being corrupted by its deceitful desires; to be made new in the attitude of your minds; and to put on the new self, created to be like God in true righteousness and holiness" (Eph 4:20–24). Paul uses the language of taking off and putting on; clearly, he has the image of dressing and undressing in mind. Sanctification is like changing clothes; you take off an old outfit and put on a new one.

I had a friend who would often find himself in jail. For as long as I knew him, he would be in and out of one jail or another. When I heard he was back in jail, I would go and visit him, and he would inevitably come into the room where we would meet wearing orange coveralls, just like on TV. These coveralls were the apparel of the convict. They have become a symbol. They designate someone as a prisoner. Whenever I saw him outside of the detention center, he was never wearing the orange coveralls. He always had a set of normal street clothes on. Now, I was never there on the day he was released from jail, when he was given his street clothes to put on, but I am sure he did not wrestle with whether to change his clothes or just stick with the orange jump suit. I am confident that he stripped off the orange outfit as quickly as he could and donned the clothes of a free man. The coveralls symbolized incarceration; the new clothes symbolized liberation. He gladly took off the old and put on the new, because the clothes spoke about his identity. That is what Paul is saying to the Ephesians. They are liberated people, set free by the Spirit of God at work in them. Their job is to live into that liberation by giving themselves to the process of sanctification by getting rid of the stuff that keeps them back from God and his intentions and putting into their lives things that draw them to God and reflect his intentions for their lives.

Paul goes on to list, in Eph 4:25—5:17 specific behaviors and attitudes that need to be "taken off" and some that need to be "put on," so that his audience understands specifically what their lives will look like as they give themselves to the sanctification process. The key to this is made plain in 5:18 when Paul writes, "Do not get drunk on wine, which leads to debauchery. Instead be filled with the Spirit." The issue is one of control. Who or what will you submit to? Is it to that which will lead you away from God and into the things that detract from what he intends for you or even corrupts you? Or will you submit to his Spirit and be filled by him, so that your life is one of deep connection with God and the things of God (vv. 19–20). This is largely the same idea that Paul communicates in Galatians 5, when he presents a contrast between a life not centered on Christ and one that produces the fruit of a life guided by the Spirit (Gal 5:19–24). The key to nurturing the fruit of a life connected to God is to "keep in step with the Spirit" (Gal 5:25). It is to keep submitting to the promptings of the Spirit that call us into deeper trust, deeper submission, and deeper knowledge of God.

In the past, there were some who used the language of "second blessing" to describe the ongoing process of sanctification. The second blessing is tied in with the idea that we don't come into the fullness of God's Spirit until after our conversion, and we subsequently have a "crises" experience that drives us to the end of ourselves, and thus to God, where we encounter him again. I would suggest that we all need an experience like that; in fact, multiple experiences of coming to the end of ourselves and turning to God for a fresh encounter with him for our conversion is only the starting point of our Christian journey, and there is much more that God wants to do with us. We should not question whether our subsequent experience with God is legitimate, if it does not seem to meet the rather subjective criteria of "crises." In fact, subsequent to conversion, God has many new experiences for us, and we should be prepared for numerous "blessings" of his Spirit in our lives as we yield to his sanctifying work in us. But even when they are the result of spiritual, physical, family or social crises, they always include a call from the Lord to give ourselves more completely to him, and to receive him in a more complete way, to leave self, and to be filled with the Spirit.

SANCTIFICATION IS THE EXPERIENCE OF GOD'S ABUNDANCE

A final aspect of sanctification that we have already alluded to but needs to be explored more fully is the idea that sanctification leads us to the experience of God's abundance both individually and communally (i.e., as a church). Alliance spirituality has always understood that sanctification is the move into what is sometimes called "the deeper Christian life," a deeper experience of God and his intentions for our lives. This is at least part of what Paul has in view with his use of the term "life," a kind and a quality of life that is distinctly different from the kind of life offered by the world. Yielding our lives to the process of sanctification brings about a fullness of life that cannot be found elsewhere because, as we considered at the outset of this message, at its core, sanctification has to do with a relationship and its developing intimacy. If we go back to Romans 8, we can see Paul's understanding of this fact coming through clearly: "For those who are led by the Spirit of God are the children of God. The Spirit you received does not make you slaves, so that you live in fear again; rather, the Spirit you received brought about your adoption to sonship. And by him we cry *Abba*, Father" (vv. 14–15). The work of God's Spirit in us is to create and cultivate intimacy with God. He liberates us from slavery to and fear of this world and draws us into a relationship that is characterized by Paul as a close, child-parent kind of relationship. The term "Abba" is one of great endearment and so is used by Paul to describe what the Spirit comes to forge in our lives.

Sanctification, as we considered at the outset, is the act of being set apart for holy purposes, and it connects us with God's ultimate purposes for us and for human community. In the Old Testament, the word used to describe God's ultimate purpose for his people is *shalom*. *Shalom* is a word that loosely translated is "peace" but encompasses more than a lack of war or an inner contentment. *Shalom* is a term that weaves together justice and peace into a spirit-created community, where contentedness, wholeness, and blessedness is experienced and demonstrated. *Shalom* is both a private, interior reality and a communal experience, which is the ultimate goal of God's laws being practiced in the real world experience of his people. It describes a community that models the reign of God in its life together. It is a community of people who are in the process of sanctification, and as a result of their individual experience of God's transforming work, are being transformed together.

There is also another important dimension to sanctification, that is, God's deep desire to form a holy people for his missional purposes in this world. Ultimately, our sanctification is not just for our good, it is for the good of the world. As we yield to Christ's working in us and are being transformed, we engage with others who are also in this process of spiritual transformation, and we become the church. It is through our collective transformation that the *shalom* of God emerges as it is practiced.

God's sanctifying purposes take us deeper into relationship with him, but this is not just so that we might revel in knowing him better, it is also so that his kingdom purposes might be furthered. The intimacy with God that is the result of the sanctification process has tangible expression through the collective life of the church, offering the world an alternative reality. It is a reality that is rooted in the practice of God's word, always imperfectly but with authenticity and sincerity in the life of a sanctified community.

As we yield to the work of Christ's Spirit in our lives and seek to obey God's word as it comes to us through the Scriptures and the voice of the Spirit, we will increasingly experience the presence and power of God in our lives and in the church. As this occurs, the world will see an alternative community of people who have been set apart by God to demonstrate the possibilities that knowing him can make in their lives, the community in which we live, our country, and the world.

God's sanctifying purposes are directly connected with his desire to share his abundance with the world. We, the church, are the place where this begins, and our duty is to give ourselves wholly to God in yielding trust that his sanctifying work will lead us into his abundance and into the life for which he has created us.

CONCLUSION

This is why sanctification is one of our foundational beliefs as an Alliance family. It is the doctrine of Christian spirituality that leads us deeper into the purposes of God for his church. It is the doctrine that teaches us about our identity in Christ as people who are set apart for divine relationship and purposes. We are sanctified when we choose to place our faith in Jesus Christ and follow him in faith. We continue in the process of sanctification as God prompts us to change something in our lives, something that will lead us into a fuller experience of him, and we say "yes" and yield to Christ, trusting that his way is best for us. As we do this, God gives more of his Spirit to enable us and fill us, then we see the holy character of Jesus emerge a little more clearly as a result of our ongoing relationship with God and his sanctifying purposes. As we continue in this relationship, what is happening in our life individually is also happening collectively in the church as a whole, and God's shalom is offered to the world. Thus, as we consider the sanctifying purposes of God in our lives, we must realize that our sanctification transcends our own spirituality or sense of intimacy with God, as it is also for the sake of the world that God is sanctifying us.

For those of us who have been captured by the love of God and this vision of transformation that leads us into God's shalom, we understand that once we have come to Christ and received his Spirit as we continue in him, there will inevitably come a time when we will desire more of his Spirit's presence in our lives. Perhaps we will come to grips with our need for his power to overcome certain struggles with our sinful behavior or self-centered attitudes. Perhaps we will be overwhelmed by a desire to just walk more intimately with God. Maybe we will recognize our need for his power so that we can serve more effectively. Maybe difficult life circumstances will overwhelm us and cause us to struggle with God's purposes, but through this struggle, we find ourselves surrendering to him in deeper trust, even when we do not have all the answers that we seek. Over the course of our Christian journey, all of these things may rise up in our lives, perhaps even multiple times. It is this recognition of our need for more of God's Spirit that drives the process of sanctification and leads to increasing holiness in character, effectiveness in service, and experience of God.

Where are you in this divine process? What is God calling you to do in response to his work of sanctification in your life? The key to the sanctified life is always to say "yes." Whenever we offer

God a yielding "yes," his sanctifying purposes will go forward in our lives and in his church. What is he saying to you today? Will you offer him your "yes"?

DISCUSSION FORUM

On-Line Interaction on the Sermon: "Jesus Our Sanctifier"

Pastor Andrew,

In your sermon on Sunday, you didn't really address the question, "Is it possible to truly be a Christian and yet not long to be sanctified?" Isn't what you were talking about just the normal Christian life?

Bill

Hi Bill,

Sticking with the marriage analogy that I used a lot in the sermon, in some ways this is like saying, "Is it possible to be married and not long to be loved by your partner and to give love"? Many people come to Christ with one request or desire, they want their sins forgiven, or they want to be more spiritually fulfilled, and as they initially trust Christ, that request is granted. But, the Holy Spirit enters one's life and begins immediately to speak to the person who has truly become a child of God, but who does not yet understand that coming to Christ for forgiveness or fulfillment is only one part of being a child of the Great King. This speaking may turn into what some have termed as "striving" where the Spirit works in the deep parts of a person to bring them to Christ in his fullness, fanning into a flame a longing for Christ that continues and develops in a life-long process.

If there is not such a longing to be like Christ, and if a person just wants forgiveness but still wants to live as they please, that is, to continue to have themselves at the center of their life, without obedience and submission to Jesus, then it is legitimate to ask, "Is this perhaps a sign that in fact they have not come to Christ in a genuine way, that they have not truly become a Christian"? And sadly, the answer may be "yes"; such a person is not yet a true Christian. So in that sense, no, it is not possible to be a Christian and not be sanctified, and yes, sanctification is the normal Christian life. However, there is a conscious process that we must enter into and continue in, if we are to experience the work of God in our life in a deeper way.

Andrew

Hi Andrew,

Could you define what you mean by "holiness" as it pertains to the Christian life? I think that there can be a lot of misunderstanding around this word and concept. I would like to know what your thoughts are on what it means for a Christian to be "holy." Thank you!

Sharon

Hi Sharon,

I appreciate your faithful participation in this forum each week. Of course, when we discuss the issue of sanctification, the idea of holiness is part of the equation. When we come to Christ, two things happen. The Father sees us as having Christ's righteousness, as being "in" Christ. There is a sense in that when the Father looks at me, he sees Christ. This is a wonderful gift that should create gratitude in our hearts, when we happen to doubt or feel unworthy. The second thing that happens is that Christ comes to live in us by the Holy Spirit. At some point, as I said in the sermon, the Holy Spirit stirs us, strives with us, and calls us to stop living for ourselves and to give ourselves fully to him. This has sometimes been called a crisis experience, where we do step into an experience of holiness. When we say yes to the Holy Spirit, he fills us with his presence. But he will not leave us there, but will call us again to an even greater or deeper experience of holiness. This is an ongoing process. We are ever learning more about ourselves, that is, our weaknesses, our sinful leanings, and self-centeredness. The Holy Spirit keeps calling us out of that to a deeper experience of Christ that helps to move us away from our sinful inclinations. Thus, our outer behavior is transformed in a way that reflects the character of Christ more and more fully. However, it is important to understand that holiness is often misunderstood as something otherworldly, that someone who is really holy is far removed from the realities and behavior of the real world. This is false. We need to understand that experiential holiness does not mean perfection; in fact, it may look different in different people's lives. Holiness means growing in the process of sanctification, so that our everyday life experience of holiness is catching up to what we are when the Father sees us in Jesus. To be holy doesn't mean that we have arrived or been made perfect, it means we are cooperating with the work of the Spirit in our lives, and we are being transformed more and more into the character of Jesus. I hope that helps. Thanks Sharon.

Andrew

Hi Andrew,

I was challenged by your message on Sunday. I have been struggling with it ever since. So much of what you emphasized was trusting God and submitting to God, etc. I struggle with that because I have been "burned" by God in the past. I have trusted him only to find that he does not always seem to come through. Also, I have experienced some difficult times in my life, and I struggle with not questioning or blaming God for a lot of it. I really struggle with the idea of fully trusting myself in him. How do I regrow trust? Thanks.

Luke

Hi Luke,

Thanks for this question. I am glad that you took the risk to share yourself so honestly. Let me begin by affirming that you're struggle is important and that it is a sign of your commitment and sincerity in your relationship with Jesus. Now, I want to speak to you bluntly, but in love. I would submit that you have never been "burned" by God. Part of what you seem to be describing is an experience where you believed that you knew what needed to happen, where you set the standard, where you created the definition of what proper divine activity in your life should look like, and when it did not turn out the way you planned it, you considered that God had promised you something and failed, that is, you had been burned. But that is not the case. God is God, he is God overall, he creates the definitions, he sets the standards, and he does not fail in the promises he has given to us. In the same way, some of the ways you have experienced difficulty may not always be easy to understand, but we have to believe that God's character is good and that he is not responsible for the bad or evil things that occur to us. He is the God who came to us and suffered as a human being, and who identifies with our suffering and enters into our suffering in order to bring help and healing. This is what God wants to do in your life, Luke. Now, here is another blunt comment for you. Before you will be able to truly trust God, you must be humble and acknowledge your frustration with God. Humble yourself and confess that you have expected God to act according to your expectations and that you want to change that. This is the first step to developing trust again; then after that, as best as you can, commit yourself to him in trusting faith. Even if you are still not sure and are struggling with taking that step, take that first step and God will respond. This is part of the process of sanctification. It includes struggle and doubt. But clearly God is at work in you, inviting you forward. Let go of the things that are holding you back and take a step toward God and see what he can do and where you can go from here. Thanks again Luke, you have offered a very helpful question.

Andrew

Pastor Andrew,

I have asked Christ to sanctify me and to fill me with the Spirit many times, but it never fails that, within a day or two, I commit sin again. Am I doing something wrong? When I pray this way, I feel like it should have a more powerful effect, or else, maybe I am just not doing something right. Am I missing something?

Eddie

Hi Eddie,

This is a good question and obviously one that is very personal to you. Asking for the filling of the Holy Spirit and for his kind work in bringing holiness to us is a very serious thing. First, let me say that sanctification does not mean that we will no longer sin. It does not mean that our struggle is over. Sanctification is about making progress in the Christian life, growing consistently in our character and relationship with God. So it may be that you need to give yourself grace for the journey, so that you don't become too discouraged and give up on the good work God is doing in your life. However, the other side of the situation is that it may be that your commitment is not complete. Some have said that sanctification means "giving all that I know of myself to all that I know of God." So here is where I want to ask a hard question: did you give "all that you know of yourself?" Or, is there something you are keeping back, a room in your heart's home that you want to keep locked up that Jesus can't go in there—perhaps not a big room, perhaps a room you only visit occasionally, but a room for which you have the key? Ask the Holy Spirit to examine your heart for the answer to this question. Then, and only then, we can embrace the teaching on the progression of sanctification. Changing us into a holy person is something that the Lord does for us over time. When we seek the fullness of the Spirit and in his power clean up all those rooms he wants cleaned up, we begin this journey. But, it is a journey, and just as our houses require continual cleaning and repair, so also our lives must be continually examined, confess sins, and seek the power of Jesus. But, if we have truly brought Jesus to the center of our lives, then when we ask Jesus to come again and cleanse us and restore us, we are not inviting him in from the outside to "our" house, but from the inside to cleanse and restore "his" house, and we can have confidence that he will do exactly that. I guess I have offered you both encouragement and a challenge here Eddie, you will have to decide which one answers your question the best. Thanks!

Andrew

QUESTIONS FOR FURTHER CONSIDERATION AND DISCUSSION: "JESUS OUR SANCTIFIER"

Why is submission to others, and even to God, a hard concept for us to embrace and live out?

How does the idea of being "set apart for holy purposes" strike you? Does it sound inviting? Scary? Unattainable? Life giving or life taking? Why does it make you feel this way?

What stops us from saying "yes" to God's sanctifying purposes in our lives?

How does the emphasis on relationship in the sermon contribute to your understanding of sanctification? How does your relationship with God differ from other relationships? How is this helpful, and how is it a challenge? The sermon draws primarily from the marriage relationship, what other principles from human relationships can contribute to our understanding of the process of sanctification?

How does the "taking off" and "putting on" analogy in Ephesians 4 and 5 give focus to the process of sanctification? What challenges does it bring? How can this be a realistic experience for us as we grow in our faith and experience of sanctification?

How does the concept of *shalom* relate to sanctification, and how does the idea that sanctification is not just personal but communal resonate with you? In what ways can your congregation be more open to the sanctifying work of the Spirit?

Biblical texts to consider: Rom 8:1–13, Eph 4:17–5:21, Gal 5:13–25

4

Jesus Our Healer

INTRODUCTION

SEVERAL YEARS AGO A woman in my church was diagnosed with cancer. The church began praying for her healing, and as things unfolded, it appeared as if she would have to have surgery. Some weeks prior to the surgery, in one of the public services of the church, at her request, some of the elders of the church anointed her with oil and prayed that God would heal her of the cancer as we are instructed to do in James 5. Shortly after this the woman went to her doctor for an appointment prior to her surgery, x-rays revealed that the cancer was no longer visible. Further tests confirmed that the cancer had disappeared and that surgery would no longer be necessary. She believes that Jesus healed her, and I have no reason to doubt that she is right about that, because if we accept the teaching of Scripture, we know that healing is something that God does. Yet, any of us who has experienced serious sickness or have known someone who has may have wondered about this claim. If God heals why does he let some suffer or struggle with illnesses of various kinds? How does healing work, and why does it often seem not to work?

As a movement, the Christian and Missionary Alliance is founded upon the concepts of Jesus our Savior, Sanctifier, *Healer*, and Coming King. As we have been exploring these ideas together, we now come to this foundational doctrine of healing. What do we mean when we declare Jesus as "our healer"? Is his healing power available for us today, and if so, how should it function in our life as a church?

DIVINE HEALING IN SCRIPTURE
AND ALLIANCE HISTORY

The biblical portrait of God clearly depicts him as the one who holds the power of life and death, sickness, and health. As such, it is no surprise that the people of Israel saw God as their healer. This fact is clearly disclosed to them shortly after their exodus from Egypt, and they find themselves wandering in the dessert. When they come upon a pool of water that is undrinkable, God miraculously transforms the water into water that the people can drink and be sustained by. At this point in their journey, God promises that, if the Israelites stay faithful to him, he will protect them from the diseases that he had brought upon the Egyptians saying to them, "I am the Lord, who heals you" (Exod 15:26).

What a promise. God declares that he is the one who holds the health of the people in his hands and that he is the one who brings us deliverance from our sicknesses. Psalm 103 reiterates the all-encompassing nature of God's sovereignty over the things that distort and detract from human life when the psalmist declares, "Praise the Lord, my soul, and forget not his benefits—who forgives all your sins and heals all your diseases" (vv. 2–3). The Old Testament picture of God offers a vision of the world in which God stands above sin and sickness and is able to deliver people from both.

Examples of God's power to heal people's sicknesses and diseases are found in the stories of Israel's king Hezekiah (2 Kgs 20:1–11; 2 Chr 32:24–26) and the story of the Aramean soldier, Naaman (2 Kings 5). The prophet Isaiah reflects the theological vision of the Old Testament's portrayal of God as healer but also begins to anticipate how it will be manifest in the life and ministry of Jesus, when he declares in Isa 53:4–5, "Surely he took up our pain and bore our suffering, yet we considered him punished by God, stricken by him, and afflicted. But he was pierced for our transgressions, he was crushed for our iniquities; the punishment that brought us peace was on him, and by his wounds we are healed." The figure that Isaiah is referring to here is often debated in terms of who his original audience may have understood this to be, but the New Testament is clear that Isaiah was pointing to Jesus. In Jesus, the work of God was manifest and this included the work of healing in all aspects of life—healing from sin and sickness and from the pain they bring to our lives.

The Gospel of Matthew makes plain the connection between God as healer and Jesus as healer. Matthew 8 offers three stories of Jesus' healing power. First, in vv. 1–4, Jesus heals a man with leprosy, then in vv. 5–12, Jesus provides healing for the servant of a Roman centurion. These are followed in vv. 13–14 by Jesus' healing of the mother-in-law of one of his disciples. After these three stories, we read, "When evening came, many who were demon-possessed were brought to him and he drove out the spirits with a word and healed all the sick." Then Matthew adds this comment: "This was to fulfill what was spoken through the prophet Isaiah: 'He took up our infirmities and bore our diseases.'" Matthew joins the vision of Isaiah with the work of Jesus, offering to his readers and to us the idea that Jesus came to do the work of God, which includes the ministry of healing.

Of course the three stories in Matthew 8 are only a small sampling of the ways that Jesus is depicted in the four Gospels as a healer. The stories that assert and reinforce this idea are too numerous to list at this point. What is essential for us to grasp is that Jesus embodies the work of God. The God who is revealed in the Old Testament as a God of healing is found doing that very work in the ministry of Jesus.

While we can certainly understand that God is able to heal, and Jesus as God's son is also able to heal, what about the church? How is the healing work of God through his son Jesus Christ continued through the church? The answer to this question is made abundantly clear as we read the book of Acts and find that the early church both anticipated divine healing and participated in its enactment. Acts 3 tells a story of the healing of a lame beggar. The story involves Peter and John, two of Jesus' disciples but reads very similar to any number of healings that Jesus himself performed in the Gospels. The significance of the early churches' healing ministry is reported by the book of Acts in 5:12–16, where we are told that the apostles performed many signs and wonders and that people brought the sick to them in order to be healed, and "all" of them were indeed healed (v.16). The early history of the church demonstrates how the ministry of healing remained crucial to the work of God through his people. In fact, 1 Cor 12:9 tells us that some even have been given a special gift of healing to use for the benefit of others. Further, the book of James casts a vision for the ongoing practice of the ministry of healing as the church matured beyond the age of the apostles. James writes these words to the church: "Is anyone among you sick? Let them call the elders of the church to pray over them and anoint them with oil in the name of the Lord. And the prayer offered in faith will make them well; the Lord will raise them up" (Jas 5:14–15). This passage reflects the expectation that the God of healing had a continuing interest in his people trusting him to heal them when faced with sickness. The apostle James was filled with faith that God would do this work, if the church would be willing to engage in the ongoing ministry of healing as part of its overall work in this world.

As I already mentioned, this same kind of faith and expectation is part of the Alliance's identity, because it was part of the experience of our founder, A. B. Simpson. Simpson was a man who perpetually experienced ill health. When he was fourteen, he was bedridden for an extended period when his whole nervous system collapsed. A few years later, during his first pastorate in Hamilton, Ontario, he suffered a collapse so severe that he had to cease his pastoral duties for a time. Throughout his life in early adulthood, he was handicapped by numerous physical maladies. He stated himself that, for years, he labored with the help of "constant remedies and preventives." He joked about the many times he was ministering at a grave side and felt as if he would do well to just drop into the open grave himself.[1] The reality of his frail health seemed

---

1. Tozer, *Wingspread*, 70.

to come to a head in 1881, when he was pastor of the Thirteenth Street Presbyterian Church in New York City. Simpson's heart and nerves were failing so badly that he had to stop his pastoral work and go on an extended health leave. The leave took him to Old Orchard, Maine, where there was a Christian retreat and conference center that supplied him with a place to rest. There he was exposed to the ministry of a Christian physician and preacher named Dr. Charles Cullis. Cullis had a ministry of teaching and healing that spoke deeply to Simpson. He was moved by the ministry of Cullis as both a gifted Bible teacher and advocate of Jesus as healer. At Old Orchard, Simpson heard stories of divine healing and mingled with people who claimed that these things were real, based on their own experience of divine healing. Simpson began to think, "if they can be healed why can't I?" Still he struggled with it, and so he began to study his Bible on the topic. His study convinced him that healing was part of God's work, and thus, it was available to people today. This prompted Simpson to seek the experience of healing one Friday afternoon in a grove of pine trees in the woods of Maine. There under a canopy of pine branches with a fallen tree as an altar, he sought the face of God for divine healing. In those moments he felt the overwhelming presence of Christ, so that "every fiber in my soul was tingling with the sense of God's presence."[2] He arose from his knees certain that God had healed him. He made a vow that he would accept the truth of divine healing and use the blessing of his own healing to the glory of God and the good of others.[3] In order to test the veracity of his healing a few days later, he went on a long hike up a mountain. He managed to reach the mountain peak, which was three thousand feet high. When he had scaled the mountain, the once weak, frail minister was sure that he was a new man. He said, "from that time on I have had a new heart in this breast."[4] It is historically true that from that point on Simpson never suffered serious health concerns again

2. Ibid., 79. This recounting of Simpson's experience is based on Tozer's description in *Wingspread*.

3. Ibid., 80.

4. Ibid.

until just weeks before his death many years later. His productivity as a pastor, evangelist, traveling speaker, writer, editor, and entrepreneur was staggering. His transformation was so amazing that he made the doctrine of divine healing central to his ministry from that time on.

A THEOLOGY OF HEALING

This brings us to our own time and place. What should we make of divine healing today? In many contexts, it is not a doctrine that is talked about much and is practiced even less. Should we go against that trend? Of course most of us realize that some of the people who emphasize and practice divine healing do it in a way that many of us would rather not be associated with. We see "faith healers" on TV, and it strikes us as showy and self-aggrandizing. We find their antics and their doctrines misguided and embarrassing. For some people outside of the church, that is their view of Christianity, and their view is that it seems utterly ridiculous. We are hesitant to embrace ideas that might lead us into something that looks like a spectacle more than the faithful interpretation and practice of the gospel.

While these concerns are valid, they do not address the claims of Scripture and history that God is a healing God who wants to demonstrate his love and care for us through manifestations of this truth in the lives of people. We are called to take seriously the fact that Jesus' life points us toward the God who heals, and his death and resurrection offers us the assurance that our healing has been provided for in all of the multi-faceted dimensions that healing is necessary in our lives—spiritual, emotional, and physical. The question is how do we access healing, and how do we understand the reality that we do not always experience the healing that we so desperately long for?

It seems that the key to experiencing God's healing is often, though not always, rooted in faith. I say "not always" because sometimes God works despite a complete absence of faith. I also do not want to infer that the reason people are sometimes not healed is because their faith is faulty. This is not a view that we should embrace; it is full of philosophical and theological fallacies that are not able to answer the mysteries of God's working, when pressed even in the slightest way. However, very often divine healing is connected to faith in that believing that God can and wants to heal us is the spiritual movement that we offer to God as our act of faith that opens up the possibilities of experiencing his power within us.

Matthew 8 presents Jesus as the one who provides healing as a result of his suffering and death. We often refer to this as the idea that "healing is in the atonement." This means that, by his suffering, death, and resurrection, Jesus provides the world with the potential for healing from all that keeps us back from experiencing God and his world in the way that he intends for us to experience it. This transcends just physical healing and moves into other aspects of our lives and even into other realms like relationships, societal structures, and the environment. So as we embrace Jesus' work on our behalf, we open the door to all of the possibilities that it creates. Jesus' death and resurrection are a triumph over sin, sickness, and death. He came to set the world right. The question is, do we believe it? When we say "yes," it is an act of faith that opens the way for us to experience Jesus' triumph in all of its various dimensions. Through his atoning death, we can participate in his ongoing work of setting the world right. Healing is in the atonement in that the atoning work of Jesus creates the potential for the world to be restored to what God has intended it to be. Jesus' life, death, and resurrection are the hinge events that create the potential for healing to flow into every area of the world and our lives. This is why faith is central to the reception and practice of healing in our lives and ministries.

Do you have faith that Jesus died and rose again to heal you? Can you trust that God wants to restore you spiritually, physically, and emotionally? Healing begins here. This does not mean that your faith is strong necessarily; perhaps it is quite weak. But we can begin to embrace the ministry of healing only as we have the faith to believe that Jesus has come to restore a broken world in all of its various dimensions.

The model that the book of James offers picks up on these things. Notice the impetus of the text: "Is anyone among you sick? Let them call the elders of the church to pray over them and anoint them with oil in the name of the Lord" (Jas 5:14). The onus is on the sick person to initiate the prayer for healing. This is not to say that there are times when a severely infirmed person may not need others to initiate prayer and anointing on their behalf or to say that the Lord will not honor such endeavors, but it is to draw attention to where the burden for initiating healing prayers lies, that is, in the person who is sick. Why? Because it is an act of faith to call for the elders. It demonstrates our belief that Jesus is the healer and that his life, death, and resurrection create the possibility for transformation in our bodies, minds, and souls. James rightly instructs us by giving responsibility to the sick person to call for prayer, because it is an act of faith to do so.

The next verse is also telling, "And the prayer offered in faith will make them well; the Lord will raise them up" (Jas 5:15). While scholars have wrestled with the exact meaning of this verse over the years, this verse also emphasizes faith. It reminds us that those who engage in prayer for the sick also need to have faith in the fact that healing is found in Jesus and that their faith in the work of Christ to bring healing to our world is essential for healing to flow into the lives of sick people. However, it is important to clarify that this does not suggest that there is something magical in faith or in prayer. They are signs of trust in God and his sovereign ability to intervene in a given situation. One commentator puts it well when he says, "Faith energizes prayer, but not because faith is some kind of magical power or psychic force that effectualizes the prayer. Faith is that which connects a person to God and characterizes a relationship with God. It is this relationship to the healing God that secures answers to prayer."[5]

These instructions also remind us that healing prayer is a communal practice. The elders are called not because they have special

---

5. McCartney, *James*, 255.

powers to heal or even special standing before God. Church elders are representatives of the congregation. Their work is to serve the church in leadership and act as representatives for the people that they serve. Their work in healing prayer is to bring the faith of the church to bear on the needs of the sick. Thus, in seeking God for healing, faith is exercised not just by the person who is sick but also by the whole community as they come together to support and uphold the physically needy person in prayer.

There is a wonderful story in the Gospels about a man who is paralyzed and is brought to Jesus on a stretcher by four of his friends. We do not know all of the details in terms of how these men knew about Jesus or what role the sick man played in prompting this visit to Jesus, but what we do know is that these four men carried their friend to Jesus on the stretcher and, when they had trouble getting through the crowd, they actually hoisted their friend, stretcher and all, up on to the roof of the house where Jesus was, and then dug through the roof so that they could lower their friend down through the hole in the roof that they had created and place him in front of Jesus. From there, Jesus dramatically forgave his sins and healed him (Mark 2:1–12; Luke 5:17–26). This is a great picture of how healing works in the life of a local congregation. It is a communal effort where the sick person calls for help, and the church rallies together in faith that Jesus can do something as we bring the sick person to him in prayer. This is where communal faith merges, and we trust Jesus together for the work of healing.

Of course all of this raises the question, "why is it that often times God does not heal"? After all, James seems pretty optimistic here, doesn't he? All of this stuff about God as the God of healing and Jesus as our healer paints a pretty hopeful picture. Why is it that our experience of healing often falls short of the expectations we are called to have by the biblical text?

It would not be right to pretend that there are easy answers to this question. However, if we are to believe, based on the teaching of Scripture and the experiential evidence that is available— that God is a God of healing, then we do have to wrestle with the question as to why God does not heal all the time when we seek him for this gift?

One reason may be that our sickness is something that can actually have a positive impact on ourselves and on others. Sometimes God uses sickness in order to draw us closer to him and shape us more fully into the image of Christ. I have talked to numerous people, who have walked through the valley of ill health, and who have testified to me both while they were suffering and/or after they have been made well again, that the time of sickness they experienced became a period of great spiritual growth. They depended more fully on God and found his sustaining strength to be sufficient in powerful ways. In the midst of terrible circumstances, God became more present in their lives than ever before. This is what the apostle Paul is saying when he writes in Romans 8:28–29: "And we know that in all things God works for the good of those who love him, who have been called according to his purpose. For those God foreknew he also predestined to be conformed to the image of his Son, that he might be the first born among many brothers and sisters." Sometimes a time of sickness can be the time in our lives where we become more attentive to the Lord, and thus, he does things in our lives that he could not do otherwise.

Perhaps another reason that God does not heal us is because our sickness can be useful to others. Again Paul reminds us of an important spiritual truth when he writes, "Praise be to the God and Father of our Lord Jesus Christ, the Father of compassion and God of all comfort, who comforts us in all our troubles, so that we can comfort those in any trouble with the comfort we ourselves have received" (2 Cor 1:3–4). While this may not answer some of the deepest questions that we have about God's sovereignty in healing, it does remind us that our suffering can have meaning as we are able to relate to others who are sick and be of genuine comfort to them in their suffering. We all know that there is a depth of compassion that comes from someone who has been in the same kind of pain that we find ourselves in. A woman who has experienced a miscarriage can relate to another woman who has experienced the same thing in a way that someone who has never been through that experience cannot. A cancer survivor can relate to someone who has just received a bad diagnosis in a much deeper way than someone who has not experienced that disease. It could be that our battle with ill health, be it physical or mental, is something that God will redeem rather than heal. He will make us into instruments of comfort to others who are suffering or will suffer as we have.

Finally, it could be that God does not heal because sickness can be a vehicle through which he brings glory to himself. I knew a woman who was stricken with multiple sclerosis early in her middle age. She ultimately ended up in a wheel chair and was highly dependent on others. Despite many prayers for healing, her condition worsened. However, through her years of decline and in the times of hospitalization, her faith and strength of character shone through. She radiated joy, love, and graciousness to those around her—not that she never cried or got frustrated, but she was very honest about her struggles with her condition and consistently demonstrated an unwavering faith and passion for Christ. Needless to say, her circumstances and situation spoke eloquently to numerous people. Through her example, she encouraged fellow Christians to believe in the sustaining power of God, and she challenged non-believers to consider the reality of Christ. God used her sickness to bring glory to himself in a way that drew others to him.[6]

CONCLUSION

While we must accept that God does not always answer our pleas for healing, we must also embrace the fact that sometimes he does, and that we are invited to come to him and trust him for his healing touch in times of sickness. God can heal, and he does intervene and perform miracles that change circumstances and restore broken lives. When we come to Jesus, we are coming to the one who

6. It is worth noting that, after many years of being bound to a wheelchair, my friend experienced a measure of healing and was able to walk and enjoy a level of freedom that she had not had for many years. This improvement in her condition lasted for a sustained period.

came to bring wholeness to our world, a wholeness that includes the spiritual, emotional, and physical dimensions of our lives. If you have a need, he invites you to bring it to him in trusting faith that he is able to minister to your need. Will you do that? Will you come to him as your healer? Will you trust him today with those things in your life that need his healing touch?

DISCUSSION FORUM

On-Line Interaction on the Sermon: "Jesus Our Healer"

Hi Pastor Andrew,

Thank you for your sermon yesterday. I often have wanted to ask for prayer for healing, but I am afraid that I won't have enough faith to be healed. Can you offer me any guidance on how to understand what I should do about this? Thank you for considering my question.

Sincerely,

Grace

Hi Grace,

I understand your struggle. I too have had to wrestle with similar questions. In the book of Acts, the apostle Paul looked at a crowd of people and saw a lame man and discerned that the lame man had faith to be healed. What does that mean? What did that man possess that made Paul confident in his faith? What does it mean for you to have enough faith to be healed? It doesn't mean that you should do ridiculous things, such as go off your medications or stop going to your physician before you know that you have been healed. I think that what it means, that is, to have the faith to be healed, is that we have to trust the fact that Jesus is the same today as he was when he lived on earth and healed people then—that is, that he does have the authority and power and that it is his will to heal people. However, perhaps, as I mentioned in the sermon, there are reasons for healing not to take place. These are mysteries and are the things that must be searched out in prayer and reflection. But, I think that we should begin with the assumption that Christ desires our healing, and we should act on that assumption in faith. I think this is what it means to "have enough faith." Then we only come to the conclusion that, for whatever reason, we are not going to be healed after seeking it in prayer. So Grace, I would encourage you to come to the throne of mercy with confidence; the Great Physician is there for you.

Andrew,

Can you explain your view on healing in relation to things like mental handicaps, faulty vision, and other things, which do not seem to change no matter how much people are prayed for? Thank you.

Dell

Dell,

Thanks for the question. That is a tough one. Jesus, in speaking to an audience about the ineffectiveness of worry, reminded them that they could not add an inch to their height. While Jesus meant it as a reminder that God is the one who is in control of all things, it is also a subtle reminder that every person is designed a certain way by our Creator, and this design forms the frame, so to speak, in which we live our lives. We are given a certain level of intelligence, we might desire more, but we must live with how we are born. We are given certain athletic potential, and it may not be as much as we want. This applies to many things that we could mention. There are times when, for purposes known only to him, the Lord dramatically changes one or more of these parameters and thus changes a person's life; and we give God glory for that, the example of the healing of the man born blind (John 9) is one of those instances. He was born blind for the glory of God, which seems to mean that he was born blind so that he might be healed. In other cases, God's glory can be seen in the faith of the sick person, as I mentioned in the sermon. Perhaps his glory is found in the way that he gives strength to the afflicted to carry on despite their physical challenges. There are other ways that God is glorified in the lives of people whose faith is strong and whose life is an example to those who do not contend with their particular struggle, and we must also see the wisdom and love of God at work here also. At the end of the day, there is no clear answer to your question, and we have to be willing to live with this mystery.

Hey Andrew,

This may be a strange question, but what if I have great faith that God can heal me, and I experience his healing many times, is it possible that will I never die?

Nick

Nick,

Sorry to tell you, but we are all going to die. Actually divine healing is a sign of the life to come, a reminder that God has and will overcome all sickness and disease. But like the rest of the good news, it has implications for the "now" (i.e., God heals people in this world), but it ultimately is for the "still to come" (God's ultimate healing in the age to come). In this life, all of us at God's determined time must cross the river into that new land. Thanks Nick!

Andrew

Dear Pastor Andrew,

I have heard that some modern medicines, such as vaccinations, may be harmful. If healing is a genuine possibility, should I live without medicine and simply trust God with my health?

Wanda

Hi Wanda,

Thanks for this. When it comes to this issue, I have been guided by the wisdom I once heard from another pastor who told the story about how he suffered greatly from intense headaches. He sought healing, and indeed the headaches were relieved to the point that every now and then he would get a headache, but of a low enough intensity that taking an aspirin would alleviate it. However, he felt guilty, because he thought that taking an aspirin was a sign of a lack of faith. One day he sensed the Lord ask him, "Can you take this aspirin as a gift from me and offer the same thanks to me that you give before you eat a sandwich?" This was a powerful word to him, and he responded to it by saying, "yes." This story has guided me greatly. God has given us food and has also provided many things that combat infections and disease. We should receive all of these with thanksgiving as part of the way he provides for our needs. I hope this helps answer your question. Thanks again, Wanda.

Andrew

Andrew,

As an elder, when I pray for healing for the sick, I am always careful to say, "if it be your will." I don't want to build false expectations for people, and I don't always know for sure what it is that God wants to do with a person. Is this a practice I should continue? Thanks Andrew.

Sam

Sam,

I appreciate this question, because what you are describing is a very common practice, at least in my observation. As you know, Jesus prayed to his Father in Heaven that, if it were possible for the cup of suffering—his arrest, the beatings, and the cross—to pass from him, but then he went on and prayed, "nevertheless, your will be done." We should always want God's will to be done when we pray. When we pray for healing, we must never demand from God as if we can control him. However, on the other hand, we should boldly claim the promises of the word of God. The great church reformer in the sixteenth century, Martin Luther, said that we should take the whole sack full of promises that we find in the Bible and shake them out at God's feet. That is, we should claim those promises and not be afraid to remind God that he made them to us. So don't let "if it be your will" become a "hedge" just in case there is no healing, even worse, don't let it become a cloak for actual non-belief. Instead, believe truly and assume sincerely as you pray that God does desire to heal and that he is able. In this way, your heart is an open road for the delivery of a miracle. We should always want God's will to be done, but as an elder, when you pray for the sick, surrender to the ultimate purposes of God but believe that God wants to heal the person you are praying for.

Andrew

QUESTIONS FOR FURTHER CONSIDERATION
AND DISCUSSION: "JESUS OUR HEALER"

Have you ever experienced physical healing? Have you ever known someone who has? Tell the story(s).

Do you wrestle with the idea that God is a God of healing? If so, why? Do you struggle with questions about healing? If so, what are some of the questions you have? How do the various reasons for why sometimes God does not heal help address (or not) some of your questions?

How does the character of God and the ministry of Jesus inform your own understanding of healing, and in what way, if any, is it a cause for you to wrestle with the doctrine of healing?

How does the experience of A. B. Simpson as described in the sermon strike you? How does it challenge you? What do you find helpful or unhelpful about it?

What is your experience of the ministry of healing in the church? How have you seen it practiced or not practiced? How have you seen it mis-practiced? How has it been well practiced?

What is the role of faith in divine healing—the sick person's faith, the elders' faith, the church's faith? How does what is presented in the sermon help in your understanding of these questions (if anything)?

What stops people from seeking God's healing in their lives? How can the church address some of these things in order to help people seek God for healing?

Biblical texts to consider: Isa 53:4–5; Matt 8:1–17; Acts 5:12–16; Jas 5:14 –15.

5

Jesus Our Coming King

INTRODUCTION

OVER THE YEARS MANY people have predicted the date that
Jesus would return to earth. In 500 CE, a trio of prominent
Christian leaders predicted that Jesus would return that year. In
the 1500 years that have transpired since then, dozens of notable
people, with varying amounts of actual credibility have cited a year
and a day that the world should expect Jesus' return. Recent history has provided us with a steady stream of confident forecasts,
assuring us that Jesus will return on or around a specific day and
time. If history teaches us anything, it is that we can pretty much
be assured Jesus will not return on the date that someone has predicted he will!

While trying to predict the exact date of the second coming
has proven to be a bit of a fool's game, the doctrine of Christ's return
is a foundational one for much of Christianity. As a movement, the
Christian and Missionary Alliance has been no exception to that
rule, the concept of "Jesus Our Coming King" is one of the core
ideals that has defined our identity since the Alliance's inception.
While it is probably best to refrain from predicting exact dates, we
believe in the idea of Christ's "imminent" return. This term has a
certain amount of theological baggage attached to it, but perhaps
it is best understood as a way to describe the fact that Jesus' return
is impending or bound to happen. It is something that the believer
should always be ready for.

Of course many of us realize that this doctrine does not come without a number of negative images attached to it. For many of us, when we think of the idea of Christ's return, we may think of the *Left Behind* book series that was popular a while ago or the kind of Hal Lindsey's inspired assurances that this world will ultimately meet a fiery end, and its citizens will land in the hands of an angry God who would condemn the vast majority of them to an eternity of torture and torment. Lindsey was an end-times prophecy guru who was particularly popular in the 1970's and 80's. He and other "end-times experts" like him presented this gloomy vision in a way that was usually filled with certainty that the time for this catastrophic end was close at hand. The horrific picture that was painted as a result of Jesus' return left many of us preferring to ignore end-times rhetoric altogether. It seems murky and scary, and quite frankly, not very hopeful. Yet, try as we might, we cannot escape the fact that the Bible clearly presents Jesus as returning to earth in order to bring this present age to a close and establish a new one.

However, are we stuck with adopting the understanding of Christ's return in the way that it has traditionally been taught in much of the evangelical church over the past half-century? How should we understand this doctrine of Scripture, and can we truly embrace the hope that is supposedly offered through it?

JESUS AS OUR COMING KING

As already mentioned, the return of Christ is a theme that reoccurs throughout the New Testament. Jesus himself promised it (Matt 24:30; Mark 13:26), and it is found throughout the teachings of the apostle Paul (1 Cor 15:23–24; 1 Thess 4:13–18). Further, in 1 Peter, we also see this doctrine emphasized. The author makes note of Jesus' return or the idea of the culmination of the present age numerous times throughout his short letter (e.g. 1:5, 7, 13; 2:12; 4:7, 13; 5:1, 4). It is not hard to understand why the hope of Christ's return would be emphasized in the New Testament in general and 1 Peter in particular, when the early church was a group of people who by and large were a people of suffering. Peter is explicit about this throughout his letter, specifically, in 4:12 he refers to their circumstances as akin to a "fiery ordeal." Their sufferings as a result of their faith is a key theme in the letter, so Peter is inclined to remind them that there is an end in sight, a time when Jesus will come back and set the world right again. For an audience that was not experiencing a life of prosperity and ease, such a message was certainly a welcome note of hope.

For those of us who live in the relative comfort and safety of the Western world this message may not be as compelling. Most of us do not experience persecution for our faith; we live in comfortable circumstances and have opportunities that many can only dream of. Further, we have dreams for our future, and we want the chance to see them fulfilled and uninterrupted by the return of Christ. I remember even as a young preacher that I did not want Jesus to return too soon. I was excited to get out there and grab my piece of the action, have some adventures, get married, enjoy some success, and live out some of my dreams. This is the hope of most North American young people—to pursue their ambitions and to engage in various experiences that life promises. Additionally, we believe in progress. While the world surely has its problems, we live under the modern idea that we can solve these problems ourselves. Technology is advancing at a rapid rate, and medical discoveries are new every day; therefore, we are no longer convinced that we need dramatic divine intervention in the form of Jesus' return to actually set things straight. It looks like we might be able to take care of that ourselves, thank you very much! For many of us, the return of Christ is not something we are desperate for, because the lives we live are relatively happy, and our problems are usually solvable one way or another.

Yet, we are also aware that our reality is not everyone's reality. The progress that we so deeply believe in has not ended war and famine; it has not alleviated child sex-trafficking or spousal abuse. Children live on the garbage dumps in Sao Paulo, Brazil. Sickness and death still plague us. While most in North America may not face persecution for their faith, millions in our world do. Even driving through the inner cities of our urban centers reminds us of how life in this world is not comfortable for large segments of our populace. The world is in disrepair for many, even if it is pretty good for some of us. However, even those of us whose lives are relatively settled, if we are realistic, we realize that terrible suffering could be just around the corner. The truth of this world's harshness is only a bad diagnosis or a terrible accident away. The reality of our world's brokenness is the reality that Jesus' second coming addresses. If we are honest, we all realize that the deep, wretched problems of our world are beyond our control. We cannot figure them out to the point that we can alleviate human pain and suffering. To this dilemma, God offers the hope of Jesus' return to set things right. The kingdom is in disrepair and is awaiting the return of the king to restore it to its intended glory. But what does that mean, and what does it look like?

THE SECOND COMING AND ITS
IMPLICATION FOR THE CHURCH

1 Peter offers its readers the assurance that the current disorder of things is moving toward its ultimate demise (4:7a). However, the author of this epistle is not interested in exploring the time or way that Christ will return or what needs to happen before it occurs. For Peter, the importance of the second coming is that it calls for a response from the people of God. Thus, Peter lays out a number of implications that should result when you live in hope for Christ's return.

Prayer

After offering assurance that the end of all things is near, Peter calls his readers to "be alert and of sober mind so that you may pray" (4:7b). This is an admonition to stay engaged in the world and to stay active in faith. Remaining alert and of sober mind is an admonition to not run away and retreat from what is going on around us. Rather, we are to stay aware of our circumstances, keeping ourselves rooted in the realities of life so that we can pray and intercede effectively on behalf of our world. Prayer is an act of faithful engagement. It is an activity that is rooted in awareness of need. You cannot pray effectively unless you know what needs to be prayed for, and Peter here is calling his churches in Asia Minor to stay alert to their realities, so that they can pray intelligently. It is also a call to faith keeping in that, while there may be real trials in the world, even events and happenings that may tempt you to wonder if God is really in control, prayer is the activity that keeps us engaged with God and expresses our faith that he is indeed in control; and thus, we can bring our intercessions before him in the belief that it makes a difference.

The second coming is not a doctrine that should make us blasé about life in this world. Rather, according to Peter, it should keep us vigilant about the circumstances around us and occupied in the work of intercession on behalf of the needs that we see.

Love

The second thing Peter tells his churches in light of the coming end is that they need to "[A]bove all love each other deeply, because love covers over a multitude of sins" (4:8). Love is a key theme in 1 Peter (e.g. 1:22; 3:8), and something the author took to heart from being with Jesus (John 13:34–35). Here he applies it to his readers as an appropriate response to the fact that this world as we know it is coming to an end. He makes clear that their deep love for one another has the power to overcome many sins. Why would Peter raise that point? It is true that love does help others to forgive us our mistakes. Once I forgot it was Valentine's Day. My wife waited well into the evening for me to produce a present or some flowers, a card, or at least a verbal "Happy Valentine's Day" wish. When it became clear to her that nothing was forthcoming, she jogged my memory by giving me a beautiful card assuring me of her love for me (at least up to that point!). I sheepishly had to admit that the occasion had escaped my attention, and I promised to make it up to her. She graciously assured me that our marriage would remain intact and that there was no need for a rain check on Valentine's celebrations. Well, this incident speaks clearly to my wife's good nature; it also speaks to how genuine love covers times of short-coming. My wife could easily overlook my failure to produce gifts or cards on a culturally generated occasion like Valentine's Day, because she had consistently received affirmations of it and had a clear assurance that my love for her was firm.

While I admit this is a rather trivial illustration of the way love covers over sins (or mistakes), it does point to the reality that, when love is active and present, it can help alleviate some of the pain of sin and the suffering that ensues. Peter's call to love one another is a call to bring the love of Jesus that addresses human fallenness to bear on the difficult circumstances that people, be-lievers and non-believers, face in this world. Tangible expressions of Christ's love to one another brings comfort, grace, and sustain-ing strength into the harsh realities that this world metes out. In that way, it covers over the pain of this world's sins and sustains us as we wait for the better day that Christ's return will usher in.

Hospitality

From here, Peter seeks to engender in his churches another re-sponse to the ultimate end of things. As they await the end of this age, they are to "[O]ffer hospitality to one another without grum-bling" (4:9). In ancient Mediterranean culture, hospitality was an important practice. To welcome people to your table was to offer them a type of family inclusion. It was for them an offer of esteem and status in your home.[1] The call to hospitality was a call to live out Christian character and offer the kind of grace to one another that God has offered us (4:10). Simply put, Peter is telling his read-ers to take care of each other by cultivating their communal life. Their sharing of hospitality is a counter experience to their experi-ence of persecution and hardship in the world. As they make a

1. Green, *1 Peter*, 145.

place for one another in their homes and at their tables, they are reminded that they have a place where they belong, where they are loved, and where there is friendship and encouragement rather than hostility and abuse. Their sharing of hospitality was a sign of the way things are supposed to be, rather than the way that they often are.

Serve One Another

Finally, Peter encourages his people to, "use whatever gift you have received to serve others, as faithful stewards of God's grace in various forms" (4:10). The coming return of the Lord should provoke us to service, using the various gifts that God has given to each of us to the good of others.

I once heard a story that may or may not be true, but it told of a small church that had a tradition when people were baptized. They would often have their baptismal services at a river nearby, and after the new converts were baptized, the people of the church would gather around them and offer encouragement in the form of tangible offers for service. One woman would tell the new members how much she loved children, and if they needed babysitting, she could be counted on; one of the men offered his services as a mechanic; another member told of their passion for cooking and assured those who had just been baptized that, if they ever found themselves in need, she would be there with a meal or three. It went on like that for several minutes as members of the church offered their gifts in service to one another. Apparently, in that town they have a word for that kind of sacrificial service—they call it "church."

For Peter, the looming culmination of things precipitated by the return of Christ calls for this kind of response from the church. It is an active commitment to serve, pray, love and offer hospitality. Perhaps this might seem odd to you. Why does Peter choose these ideas for his congregations? Shouldn't the end of all things spur on something more dynamic? Isn't something more required than engagement in behaviors that are supposed to be what we do all the time anyway? Why is this Peter's injunction to churches who take seriously the return of Jesus and await its happening?

THE NATURE AND PURPOSE OF
CHRIST'S RETURN

In actuality, Peter's instructions are a reflection of his and the other Bible writers' understanding of what it was they were anticipating in the return of Christ. Their eschatological vision was that Jesus would come and consummate his kingdom on earth. Evil would be vanquished, the empire of this world would be undone, and the life of the kingdom would prevail. So in Peter's mind, by calling his church to the practices of prayer, love for others, hospitality and service to one another, he was calling them to act like an eschatological community. He was inviting them to embody kingdom life in a tangible way in this present time with the anticipation of the kingdom life coming in its fullness when Jesus returns.

While the return of Jesus and the end of the world as we know it does inevitably include God's judgment, and there are places in the New Testament that indicate that this judgment will be severe for some, ultimately, what the second coming will offer is the restoration of creation. It is not the fiery end of planet earth that some prophecy pundits predict, but it is rather the return of God's good creation to its intended state.

Perhaps for some of us this idea of a renewed creation is very different than what we have been taught. Frequently, the teaching we have received on the second coming has offered the picture of heaven as a non-material space that is occupied by purely spiritual beings. However, the vision that is presented in both testaments of the Bible seems to offer something different from this. In the Old Testament, the prophet Isaiah declares, "See, I will create new heavens and a new earth, the former things will not be remembered, nor will they come to mind" (65:17). From here, Isaiah sketches a vision of people laboring and enjoying the bounty produced by the work of their hands, and the wolf and the lamb feeding together (Isa 65:25). This is corroborated by John in Rev 21:1:

"Then I saw a new heaven and a new earth, for the first heaven and the first earth had passed away." Rather than being a place where people are taken up to, heaven is a place where God comes down to dwell (Rev 21:3). Christ's return ushers in not so much an otherworldly sanctuary that has little resemblance to the world that we currently inhabit, rather it is a new earth that provides a place for true homecoming.

The hope of Christ's return is found in the truth that we will once again enter back into a restored creation that is the home that we have longed for. This truth is rooted in a vision of creation that views this world as intrinsically good. This is in opposition to the view held in many quarters that understands creation as "evil" and heaven as "good."[2] Thus, Christ's return is not ultimately rooted in destruction but in restoration. It is a vision of renewal that recognizes the world's fallenness but also its beauty and potential for goodness. It affirms that this world as it currently stands is not our home, but it also affirms that God's creation is not ruined beyond repair, it is simply in need of the kind of renewal that Jesus will bring in his return. And as 1 Peter makes clear, this new creation is a home that is distinct from the original one in at least one clear way—that is, it is an inheritance that will not "perish, spoil, or fade" (1:4).

The revelation of this inheritance is rooted in God's work of redemption, which brings with it the restoration of God's original intent for his creation.[3] With the return of Christ, human history culminates, and a new creation begins, where once again God is present and his will is done. It is a place where both the first-century audience that 1 Peter is addressing and we can be at home once again, because it is the place where Jesus Christ is ultimately revealed (1:7) and where God dwells.

The idea of our eschatological hope being the renewal of creation also fits 1 Peter's view on eschatology as being a motivation for engaging in the world right now. The language of the epistle does not speak of salvation as escape from or abandonment of this life. Instead, Peter's focus is on the promises that God offers for

2. Wright, *Surprised by Hope*, 95.

3. Middleton, *New Heaven*, 76.

the future. Peter wants his audience to understand that what is to come in the future now casts its shadow backwards, affecting the life and work of the church in the present and thus offering a way of shaping its current identity.

For the author of 1 Peter, eschatological hope is not dissociated from living a life that is engaged in the pursuit of making this world better. This may in fact be the case, because he understood the link between the current creation and the renewed creation that is to come. Future hope is inextricably linked with present hope. When 1 Peter refers to the "end" of all things in 4:7, he uses the Greek word *telos*. While this word can connote the idea of termination, it also can carry the idea of fulfillment, or "the goal to which a process is being directed."[4] For Peter, like most of the New Testament writers, the church of the first century was living in the end times, but that end had not yet come. It was now, but it was also not yet. Thus, Peter calls his audience to live in the "now" as a reflection of what life will be like in the "not yet." This was a call to subvert the normal practices of this world by offering a radical communal life that pointed to what life is intended to be, and ultimately will be, when Jesus returns. Peter's vision of the second coming is hope-filled, because it includes both present and future dimensions. He captures both the present and future aspects of eschatological hope in a way that emphasizes the fact that there is a future hope for God's people that is tied to a decisive act of Christ returning and restoring fallen creation, along with the perspective that what we do in the world right now matters and contributes to the day of ultimate homecoming.

CONCLUSION

We are all well aware that this world is far from perfect and in need of repair. As humans, we cast about for solutions; perhaps science will bring an answer, or maybe greater economic equality will close the financial gap between first- and third-world countries

---

4. Green, *1 Peter*, 141.

and improve life's condition, or maybe the next election will produce a new government that will really solve problems (though probably very few of us hold out much hope for this one). But deep down we know that we are stuck—not stuck in the sense that we can't improve things or make positive changes in various places, but stuck in the sense that we know that this world will always be filled with problems. No invention of science, no economic turnaround, no government policy will bring heaven to earth. Only Jesus himself can do that, and that is the faith that we cling to as Christians—that there is a day to come when this world will be set right, and when God will establish a new order that is rooted in and governed by his eternal righteousness and goodness. This is the age to come, inaugurated by the visible return of Jesus to this earth.

While many of the logistics of this doctrine remain a mystery, it serves as the ultimate hope of the Christian, and it is a central message of the Christian and Missionary Alliance. And, as we have already considered, it is a hope not only for our future but also for our present lives. The return of Christ calls us to live a life dedicated to serving the purposes of God's eschatological vision in the here and now. We are called to live as a reflection of the kingdom that is to come, in the midst of all of the realities of life in this imperfect world.

Historically, for the Christian and Missionary Alliance, the doctrine of the second coming has always been intertwined with the mission of the church. The imminent return of Jesus is an impetus to preach the gospel to a lost world that needs to be prepared for his coming. The Alliance has taught, based on Matt 24:14, that the evangelism of the world's people is tied to Jesus' return and that the mission of the church is key to "bringing back the king." At its very essence, our movement has always understood that the meaning of the second coming has great implications for today. The eschatological hope of Christ's return should cause us to be engaged in bringing the hope of Christ to the here and now. Jesus is coming again, but by the Holy Spirit, Jesus is here with us now, calling us to be a witness to his "now, and not yet" kingdom. The church's life as a community and our individual participation in that life is a sign of what is to come. We live in hope, but we are also dealers in hope, waiting for the day of his return and, in the meantime, living as a testimony that invites people to enter into the hope of his return for themselves. Let the hope of Christ's return inspire us to live in a way that invites others to become participants in God's kingdom in both the "now, and the not yet."

DISCUSSION FORUM

Questions and On-Line Interaction on the Sermon: "Jesus Our Coming King"

> *Hi Pastor Andrew,*
>
> *In your sermon yesterday, you emphasized the need for the second coming to be an impetus for how we live in the "here and now" and how we are supposed to reflect the values of the kingdom in our lives today in anticipation of what is to come. If living today is a rehearsal for life in the age to come, does the way that we live today change or affect the world to come?*
>
> *Sharon*

Hi Sharon,

Thanks for another good question. What you are asking reminds us that "the world to come" is a bit of a mystery, and we don't know with certainty what it will be like and how our actions in this world may or may not affect what is to come. However, the world to come is a world ruled by king Jesus, and we will work in that world. It is not an immaterial world but the world God created, which we failed to bring to its fullness of glory, but which will be brought to its fullness of glory, for it will be a world without sorrow, where the hurts of the nations will be healed and where there will be no more tears. It is easy to think that we should just sit back and wait for this world with a "who cares" attitude toward damage and distress in nature and brokenness and sorrow in people. But, we believe that some of the blessings of that world can be experienced now. In that world, we will be completely holy, and even though we are not completely holy now, we can experience the power of the Holy Spirit over sin. In the coming age, we will have perfect bodies, but even though we do not have perfect bodies now, Christ does heal. In the same way, we must work now for the healing and restoration of our world as a sign of the coming age. We work to restore nature, even though its complete restoration is in the future. We seek to rescue people from injustice, even though the reign of justice is yet to come. In so doing, we help bring the healing, restoration, and justice of the future kingdom of king Jesus to bear in our world today. In this way, I don't think that we "change" the world to come, but we change this world with the vision of the world to come. Thanks again for you question, Sharon.

Andrew

Hi Andrew,

Thanks for the message on Sunday. It definitely made me think a bit differently about the return of Christ. My question is, what role does social justice play in the world to come? Will everything just be made right and we won't have to worry about justice anymore, because it will just happen, or is there still going to be a need for us to work at making sure that people are treated justly? Thanks Andrew.

Danika

Hi Danika,

Generally, we tend to think that in one swoop, when Christ returns, the whole world will be perfect. But the accounts in Revelation seem to point to a restoration that Christians are involved in even after Christ returns. Nature is restored through our work in the kingdom, and justice is established throughout the earth. Evil is deeply entrenched and empowered by Satan, but his power is removed, and so the redeemed people are able to uproot corruption and exploitation, and the anger and rage that fuel war, creating a world of beauty and peace. I think that there will still be a role for us to play in the renewal of all things even after Jesus returns.

Andrew

Hi Pastor Andrew,

Your sermon really described the second coming differently than I have heard it before. Can you explain briefly how the "this world will be burned up, and we will end up in some new celestial home" ideology became so accepted in the church? Also, can you give a bit more biblical background to the idea of a renewed creation as opposed to the idea of heaven being "other-worldly"? Thanks for your help.

Doug

Hi Doug,

The development of this thinking is complex in the history of the church. It is rooted in a lack of appreciation for the desire of God to set all things right—things that were wrecked when our parents sinned and that have been wrecked even more as human history has ground along. This wreckage includes injustice, the continual presence of warfare, the spread of dreadful diseases, and the havoc people have set loose on the whole ecosystem. God wishes to show his victory over all this result of our sinfulness, and that victory will occur when a new order is brought by the returning king. So now, we should, as said in the sermon, "live in the shadow cast by the brightness of the future." We should work now as kingdom people to bring some of the blessings of the future to this world in every part of life and creation, living in the hope that, when Jesus comes, he will give us the power to bring great renewal to the planet earth. Note these passages: Matt 19:28; Rom 8:19–22; Eph 1:10; 2 Pet 3:13; and Isa 65:17; 66:22. Ultimately, this physical planet, locked as it is in time, will end. We do not know when or how it will end, but a new heaven and earth, somehow existing in the eternal realm, will come and not pass away. Just as Jesus' resurrection body was in some ways like our current bodies, but in other ways amazingly greater and more wonderful, so also the new heaven and earth will be even greater and more wonderful, and the images of Revelation give us hints as to its glory. This also is a great hope. Thanks Doug!

Andrew

Andrew,

I have always wondered about the verse (which you mentioned in your message) that links Christ's coming with spreading the gospel. If Christ's coming is related to "finishing the task" of the Great Commission, how do we know if we are even getting close? Once we do reach the whole earth is that an immediate trigger for Jesus to return? Some further thoughts here would be really helpful. Thanks.

Nick

Hi Nick,

First, I don't think that Jesus' words were meant to offer some kind of "trigger" for his return. They are a statement about God's desire for all people to hear the gospel and an impetus for the church to spread the message around the world. This is not to say that there is not a link between world evangelization and the second coming, but I would hesitate to tie that link too literally to Jesus' words in Matt. 24:14. The time of Christ's return will always be something of a mystery to us and, as you pointed out, we can never know for sure when the work of spreading the gospel is "done." In fact, it is never done until Jesus comes again. We do not know when the task given to the church by Jesus to preach the gospel to every tribe and nation will be completed, but we know that there is still much to do. Jesus' words are meant to inspire us to stick with the task in light of his promise that, as it moves toward completion, the possibility of his return is at hand.

QUESTIONS FOR FURTHER CONSIDERATION AND DISCUSSION: "JESUS OUR COMING KING"

What is your experience with "end-times teaching"? How has the return of Christ been described to you? Has it been emphasized in your church experience or not?

Do you agree with the sermons assertion that for many in North American culture, the return of Christ is not as compelling because of the relative comfort and hope for the future that we enjoy? Are there other reasons that may make us less expectant? How does that relate to other parts of the world where life is very different?

How does the tangible vision of 1 Pet 4:7–8, as described in the sermon, relate to your own understanding of what it means to be prepared for the return of Christ? Does it challenge the way that you have often thought about the implications of this doctrine?

How does the idea of a restored creation resonate with your own assumptions of the future? How does the idea of restored creation line up with other things you have heard taught on the subject of future hope?

How can your church embody the coming kingdom in your life together? How does the idea that our involvement in God's mission have an influence of Jesus' return (Matt 24:14) inform the ministry of the church?

Biblical texts to consider: Mark 13:24–37; 1 Cor 15:23–24; 1 Thess 4:13–18; 1 Pet 4:7–8; Rev 21:1–4.

6

The Mission of the C&MA

INTRODUCTION

NOT LONG AGO I had a conversation with someone about our church's involvement in evangelism in a third-world country. This person, who is a Christian believer, asked me why we would place so much effort in trying to introduce people in that country to the Christian gospel. "Don't they have their own religion?" my friend asked. When I affirmed that they indeed do have a faith other than Christianity, my conversation partner furrowed her brow and asked with genuine curiosity, "Well, why don't you just leave them to it? Why do you bother to send people over there to change their religion, doesn't that just lead to more problems?"

In many ways, this is a fair question. In our globalized, pluralistic, politically correct world, it seems somewhat antiquated and not very tolerant to want to try and encourage people to change their religion. That is the stuff of arrogant colonialists who thought that they knew what was good for everyone and thus imposed their culture and faith on others without a care that perhaps their "victims" were doing quite fine without them. Don't we know better today? Are we not more enlightened than that? That seemed to be what my friend was getting at, when she asked me those questions. Now, in certain ways, this is not a new question; it is one that has been asked for centuries—why bother with world mission? It is an important question, because mission has always been at the heart of the church. This morning, I would like to tell you what I told my friend that day as to why I think that the church needs to be involved in spreading the gospel to every region of our world.

As we complete our series on the things that make the Christian and Missionary Alliance distinct as a family of churches, we come to the thing that perhaps defines us as a movement most clearly—our focus on mission, especially our focus on world missions. While many church groups work very hard to send missionaries around the world, we must stress that beyond any doctrinal emphasis that we may have as a movement, it is our work in the area of world mission that has set the Alliance apart more than anything else.

In fact, world mission was the organizing idea around which this movement found its initial energy. Dr. Simpson was compelled by the idea of taking the good news of Jesus to faraway places where the message had never been heard. He, along with those who were part of the initial organizing of what was then known a the "Christian Alliance," and later the "Evangelical Missionary Alliance," wanted the message of Christ's salvation, healing, and soon return to be spread to the whole world so that all people would have the opportunity to hear, respond, and receive the benefits of Christ's work on their behalf. Initially, Simpson had no interest in forming a new church denomination. He worked across denominational lines and sought to build an "alliance" of Christians who were concerned with the world and the spread of the message of Jesus. The early constitution of the Alliance clearly stated that it had no intention of causing antagonism in the various churches, but that it would embrace Christians of "every name" who wanted to participate in the cause of world mission.[1] From those days in the late 1800's until today, the Christian and Missionary Alliance has been known more than anything else as a missionary movement.

1. Niklaus, et.al., *All for Jesus*, 75.

WHY MISSION?

I can almost hear the person I just mentioned who asked me those questions respond to these developments by saying something like, "Well that was well over a century ago. Have we not progressed since then? Don't we live in a more enlightened age? Why must you see it as necessary to continue these practices?" Once again, these are good questions.

In the first book of the New Testament, the Gospel of Matthew, we read the story of how Matthew is called by Jesus to follow him. After Matthew accepts Jesus' invitation, he hosts a dinner party at his home that includes "many tax collectors and sinners" (Matt 9:10). When the religious leaders of the day complain, Jesus makes clear to them what he has come to do; he offers them his "mission statement" if you will: "I have not come to call the righteous, but sinners" (Matt 9:13b). In this encounter with a group of leaders who did not understand why a supposed holy man or religious teacher would venture into a group of people who appear to be far from the usual synagogue crowd, Jesus made plain to them that these were the very people whom he had come to reach. Jesus was a man of mission who entered the world with a strong belief that people needed to hear the message that he came to bring. Jesus' basic orientation to the world was not that everyone was fine and just needed to be left alone to their own beliefs and way of being in the world. In fact here, as in other places, Jesus makes plain that people are not "okay." They are, according to the analogy that he uses here, "sick." They need a doctor. He has come to persuade them that there is a cure for what ails them, and he is the one who brings that cure. Now it is important to understand that, in other places, Jesus makes it clear that the religious leaders are just as sick, and they also need to be healed of their blind religiosity. In today's terms, it is important for us to recognize that we are all among those "tax collectors and sinners" whom Jesus came for. What we learn from this encounter in Matthew's Gospel is that, at his very core, Jesus is concerned with world mission.

This is not surprising, because Jesus is the embodiment of God himself, and he thus is interested in the things that God is interested in, and there is little more that God is interested in than restoring his relationship with wayward human beings. The Bible is clear that, in the beginning, God created people to be in intimate relationship with him. However, as the story goes, men and women preferred autonomy from God to relationship with God. Genesis 3, a text we considered earlier in this series, narrates the story for us, but perhaps what is most striking about the narrative of Genesis 3 as it unfolds is not the dramatic departure from God that we read about in vv. 1–7, but rather what we read in vv. 8–9. In v. 8, the original couple is now well aware that something has changed, and as they begin to digest this realization, they hear God walking in the Garden; what would have previously been a pleasurable sound now frightens them, because they are aware that the relationship has changed, and so they hide from the Lord among some trees. Verse 9 is where the story takes a surprising turn, God is depicted as searching for the couple; he calls out to them, "where are you?" In the mindset of ancient Hebrew people, who first received this text, God was not, nor was he ever, limited in his knowledge of what happened in his creation. While God is depicted here in very human terms, walking in the garden seemingly oblivious to what was going on with his creation, the author and the readers of this text would not have believed for one minute that God was ignorant of the events. Rather, the author is offering a dramatic and powerful point to his readers about who God is. He is the God, who, despite the falleness of human beings, continues to pursue relationship with them. They may have turned against him, but he continues to turn toward them. They are hiding from him, but he is looking for them. The picture of God from the Garden narrative defines God as the God of mission, the God who is striving for restored relationship. This is the story of Scripture, and thus, it is no surprise that Jesus embodies this story in his incarnation. His mission to seek "the sick" is simply his embodying the mission of God.

Thus, it is also no surprise that this is the work Jesus gives his church to do. At the end of Matthew's Gospel, we see Jesus gathering his disciples and commissioning them to continue his work—the work of going into the world and making disciples of all nations, "baptizing them in the name of the Father, and of the Son and of the Holy Spirit, and teaching them to obey everything I have commanded you. And surely I am with you always, even to the very end of the age" (Matt 28:19–20). This commission is to continue Jesus' mission of proclaiming and demonstrating the good news of the gospel; his promised presence offers his ongoing endorsement of this mission to all nations.

Thus, the first reason we continue to support world mission is because it is an expression of God's heart for redemption, and it is a continuation of his mission to all humanity. Along with this, it is an act of discipleship as we obey Jesus' command to continue God's work and to seek those who are "sick" and need his healing. Jesus has not revoked his commission to the church, and he never will until the coming of his kingdom in its fullness. Thus, we must continue to fulfill it.

A second reason why world mission is necessary is because the gospel is good news in both its content and its enactment. The gospel is the message that changes the world, because it offers the hope of Christ and his kingdom to all people. The gospel describes who we are as human beings, who God is, where we stand in relation to him, how God has acted on our behalf, and what we can become. It offers a vision for renewed relationship with God and others, of the Holy Spirit's ability to lift us above our brokenness, habitual sins, addictions, and self-centeredness, of Christ's healing care for our bodies, and, ultimately, of the hope of Christ's coming, bringing the final destruction of death, the establishment of justice, and a fully restored creation.

This is a message that the world needs to hear, and a message that deserves consideration as a way for people to orient their lives. Only as the church engages wholeheartedly in its mission to the world does this message have a chance to be heard and embraced by those who need it.

Like Dr. Simpson, I am compelled by this message. Dr. Simpson always had an interest in and commitment to missions, but while he was pastoring a large Presbyterian church in Louisville, Kentucky around 1878, he had a dream. While he slept, he dreamt that he was sitting in a vast auditorium, and millions of people were sitting all around him. He describes what happened next this way: "All the Christians in the world seemed to be there, and on the platform was a great multitude of faces and forms. They seemed to be Chinese. They were not speaking, but in mute anguish were wringing their hands, and their faces wore an expression I can never forget." When he woke up he was deeply moved; he sensed the presence and power of the Holy Spirit, and he took this as God's call upon him to give his life to the cause of world mission.[2] This vision was one that was rooted in a deep sense that people in other lands need to hear about Jesus. Just like Jesus himself taught, people are not all "okay"—we all stand in need of the gospel. For Dr. Simpson, the message of salvation, sanctification, healing, and future hope that are all rooted in the unique person of Jesus Christ was what the world needed to hear and experience. It was the church's job to provide this message in word and deed to people everywhere, and thus, Simpson was determined to engage in the mission of God around the world and tried to compel as many as possible to join him.

The result of this compelling vision is that millions of people have heard and responded to the good news of Jesus. Large Alliance constituencies exist in places like Vietnam, the Philippines, Coté d'Ivoire, Peru, and many other places. People's lives are filled with purpose and hope, because of their relationship with Jesus. Sometimes, in some of these places, people live in difficult and even in dire circumstances, but they would tell you that what makes things more bearable is the fact that they have Jesus as their Lord and that they know his presence. Would it have been better to just leave them alone? I know what they would say. Further, in countries around the world, people's lives are being improved because of the church on mission. Throughout church history, the

2. Tozer, *Wingspread*, 62.

church has been responsible for engaging with the great needs of humanity; whether it was caring for the sick during times of plague, reaching out to those with leprosy, or establishing hospitals or schools, the church on mission has always been there when human need was at its greatest. This history continues to unfold as our Alliance international workers are providing education for girls in countries where this has been rarely made available. They are becoming literate and also learning practical skills, so that they can earn money to help support their families. In other places, ministries for "at risk" girls seek to prevent their being sold into a life of prostitution by educating them, giving them a skill so that they can contribute to the family, and working with parents to help them see the folly of selling their daughter. When necessary, girls are even "rescued" from their families so as to prevent them from being sold. In other places, farmers who live at the subsistence level learn how to better irrigate their crops and plant new kinds of crops that will bring about a higher yield so that they can earn a little more for their families. All of these, and many more projects like them, are the result of the Alliance's commitment to "go into all the world." Do you think those girls or the farmers that our workers deal with wish we would have just left them alone? No, they are thankful that the church is a church on mission, and the great part is that the story is continuing today and into the future, and you and I are a part of it.

The idea that the Christian message is intended to be for the whole world is a given as is the message of many other world religions. It is hard to understand how anyone would see Christianity as a "Western" thing that should under no circumstances be exported to the rest of the world. If that logic were applied to any other idea, it would be roundly condemned. Those who think that the North American (or Western) church should avoid sharing its predominant religious ideas with the rest of the world need to be challenged by the logic of such a stance. Where else would they approve of such a position? In medicine? In technology? In music and culture? Of course not. This is not to insinuate that Christianity is a North American idea, of course it is not, and we know that it is now actually stronger in other regions of the world. But since the United States, Canada, and the United Kingdom have generally been the most active in world mission, it is the church in these countries that are most often challenged for their continued commitment to sending international workers to other lands. As we have already considered, while there have certainly been horror stories of colonization and abuse, there are even more stories of the benefits of this sending that demonstrate how withholding the good news and good deeds of the gospel would diminish the quality of life in many non-Western societies.

Brian Stewart was an award winning foreign correspondent and news anchor with the Canadian Broadcasting Corporation for many years. In the height of his work in the late-twentieth century, he covered most of the major world events around the globe. Reflecting on his experience of seeing so much devastation, he said, "I've found there is NO movement, or force, closer to the raw truth of war, famines, crises, and the vast human predicament, than organized Christianity in Action. And there is no alliance more determined and dogged in action than church workers, ordained and lay members, when mobilized for a common good . . . summing up my own experience has convinced me that Christianity is best shared with others. I'm no longer one who can say I'll just do it my way."[3]

The gospel in action is the good news and good deeds of God's kingdom breaking into people's hearts and lives as the person of Jesus Christ takes up residence there. It is the possibility of personal and social transformation, and where it takes root, those who have experienced it would never wish that they had been left alone. Instead, they thank God for the obedience of the church from other lands, who obeyed Christ's call to join him in his mission in this world.

3. From an address given by Brian Stewart at Knox College, University of Toronto, May 12, 2004, entitled, "On the Front Lines." Online access: http://www.christianity.ca/page.aspx?pid=11235.

The Changing Nature of World Mission

None of this is meant to say that the work of mission around the world should remain the same as it did in Dr. Simpson's day. Nor is it to say that we should not learn from the realities of globalization and pluralism that are now ingrained aspects of our contemporary culture here in North America. In former days of world mission, it was easy to think of those from other lands as "lost," or, in the worst-case scenario, as "savages" who were far, far away from God. Today, people from those very countries that once seemed remote geographically and culturally are our neighbors and our friends. It is easy to think that Muslims are woefully misguided, when the only Muslims you know are the ones you read about in books or perhaps see on television. It is another thing altogether, when your work mate is a Muslim and when she is one of the most wonderful people you have ever worked with. This is our reality now. It was not the way the world was back then, when Dr. Simpson was dreaming dreams and founding mission societies. Should that impact our understanding of world mission? Of course it must.

One of the great things about the changes that we have experienced in the West with the "shrinking" of the world is that people of all faiths have become more familiar with other faiths. The faith of others is no longer a complete mystery to us; even if we cannot articulate the finer points of Hindu doctrine, there is a good chance that we have an acquaintance who has a Hindu background and thus have some sense of what they are like, what holidays they observe, and how their religion affects the way they see the world. This broadened understanding allows us to recognize that people of other faiths are as committed and sure about the primacy of their faith as we are about ours.

What is needed today in the work of mission both abroad and also here at home is a willingness to engage in the marketplace of ideas. Rather than coming as "experts" who have all the right ideas and know exactly how to "fix" people and even cultures as a whole, the world as it now stands in most places calls us to come not as experts but as conversation partners and servants. This means first and foremost that we come in love. We recognize that the primary thing Jesus did was to love people, especially those who held different ideas and morality than himself. He came to them in love and treated them with deep grace and respect. This included sharing the good news with them. Love is the true essence of mission, because our mission is simply an extension of God's mission, and God's mission is all about his love for the people of the world he created. Our work in mission both at home and abroad is an expression of love, and our behavior toward those we have been sent to reach must reflect that more clearly than anything else. If this is not the case, then we have failed in our mission.

From here, we also need to enter mission with humility, the kind of humility that recognizes that we can learn just as much from those we are trying to reach as we hope they can learn from us. Engaging with a Muslim, a Buddhist, or even a secular humanist may teach us more about our own faith than anything else. Through their words, we may actually come to see places where our own personal faith is flawed or where our own understandings are lacking. We may learn of spiritual practices that could be useful in our own practice of faith. Is there any merit to implementing a discipline of stopping to pray five times a day like Muslims do? This is not to insinuate that we all should be doing that, but it is just to illustrate that there are things other faiths do that challenge our own commitments as Christians. Inter-religious dialogue opens up the potential for learning that goes both ways. We may even find that others put us to shame with their service to others. I once knew a man who was a respectful-but-avowed agnostic whose service to the poor in our community was above reproach. He loved and advocated for the marginalized in a way that put me, and most Christians I knew, to shame. His life spoke powerfully to me about things that Jesus taught and the Old Testament prophets preached. My interactions with him taught me much about justice.

Mission must be marked with the kind of humility that rejects the arrogance of colonialism or even religious superiority per se. Our evangelistic initiatives must be characterized by a genuine engagement with others that is respectful, open, and willing to learn.

This is the posture that a sending church must take as it seeks to carry out God's mission in the contemporary world. This is how we enter into the market place of ideas, whether in Edmonton, Los Angeles, Calcutta, Paris, or elsewhere. As an alliance of churches, we are still called to put mission first and still called to go into the world, but we must do it with an awareness that the context of mission has changed, and thus our methods must change too.[4]

Of course, this has deep ramifications for our national and international leaders, as well as our international workers themselves, as they have to figure out the best methods for doing mission in the place that they work. But it has ramifications for local churches in North America too, not just in how we do mission locally but also for how we support mission internationally. First, we have to address the question that my friend raised and understand why there is still a need for us to send people overseas to do ministry. As we have considered, we need to understand that the message of the gospel is needed everywhere in the world, and the good news and good deeds of the gospel contain the potential to bring light to darkness, life to death, and hope to despair. We cannot buy into the myth of our culture that it is wrong to take your faith to other places and share it. Instead, we have to believe, based on the theological ideas and practical evidence of Christianity that Jesus is the hope of the world, and thus, he needs to be declared and demonstrated in all parts of the world. Second, we have to change our own expectations of how missions are done. For those of us who have been around long enough, we have developed an idea of what "successful" missions look like. We love to hear the missionary come back from the field and talk about how many churches have been planted and how many people came to Christ. Of course these things are important, and they remain the central goals of the C&MA's mission strategy. But increasingly, our workers serve in difficult places, where progress will be inevitably slow. More and more of our workers are involved in humanitarian work that is still concerned with proclamation but also with other aspects of gospel ministry that seek to bring help to people in need as a witness to

4. Muck and Adney, *Christianity Encountering World Religions*, 27–28.

Christ's love whether or not there is an opportunity for verbal witness. In some contexts, this is the only approach that is possible. Our international workers are deeply committed to carrying out a clear witness for Jesus Christ in the places that he has sent them. But for us to think that it will look and sound the same as it did forty or even twenty years ago is to misunderstand the magnitude of the changes that have taken place in most parts of our world and in the very task of world mission. As sending churches, we must understand this and support it wholeheartedly.

CONCLUSION

Ultimately, as already noted, mission is about love. It is about following Jesus into the world and trying to love others just as he did. Thus, we proclaim the good news and demonstrate the good news as expressions of his love. This love motivates us to invite people into God's story. To help them see what God has been up to in this world, what he is still up to in this world, and how each one of us can be a part of it.

God is writing his story. In the Bible we don't have the complete version of God's story, but only part of it. It is the part we have been given to guide us as we continue that story. The story is still being written. It is the story of God's desire to redeem his creation and to restore relationship between himself and his people. It is an ongoing story in which we are participants. Every movement like the Christian and Missionary Alliance has been given the chance to write part of the story, and every local church is also given their own chapter to write. Our calling is to invite everyone that we possibly can to participate in the story. As we ourselves participate in God's mission locally and globally, we are helping to write God's story. May we continue to be a people known for our commitment to mission, and may God use us to write a powerful section of his unfolding story in the world today.

DISCUSSION FORUM

Questions and On-Line Interaction on the Sermon: "Proclaiming Jesus"

Hi Pastor Andrew,

Sometimes I wonder if the emphasis on world missions detracts or diminishes an emphasis on local missions. There are so many needs around us; shouldn't we focus on them first and foremost?

Sandy

Hi Sandy,

I appreciate your concern for our own community, but I think it is a balance of both that is needed. God has come to us in Jesus Christ, and Jesus said, "As the Father has sent me, so send I you." It is the intention of God that the Gospel be proclaimed to the whole world, and thus we cannot be content to simply work in our own church or community. God's vision for the world is much bigger and ours must be too. That said, the "whole world" does also mean people right around us who are broken under the load of sin and because of life's burdens. It is clear from church history and the Scriptures that churches are expected to fully engage with their immediate neighborhood as well as with their country and the whole world. I think this is the way the church has to be, if it is to be faithful in its partnership with God in his mission to all people.

Andrew

Andrew,

As an elder in our church, I am wondering if there is an explicit charge given to elders or church leaders in terms of their involvement in missions? Is there more expectation on leaders than on others? Thanks.

Jacqueline

Hey Jacqueline,

Glad that you are thinking through these things so conscientiously. Leadership always requires a level of commitment and accountability that may be greater than the one that is expected of others; however, the charge to take mission seriously is the same for all of us who claim to be Christ followers (Matt 28:18–20).

Now, I do believe that no person should ever be chosen to be an elder in an Alliance Church who does not deeply resonate with, does not financially support, and is not involved in this commission from Jesus, for this command is for the church, and therefore, the elders of the church are accountable to the Lord to assist in leading the congregation to carry it forward. I know that you agree with me Jacqueline; your heart for mission is clear. Thanks!

Andrew

Pastor Andrew,

I sometimes struggle with missions, because the needs and the work being done seem so far away. Is there any way that I can be more directly involved?

Wanda

Wanda,

Your question reflects a genuine reality today. We are living in an age of engagement where people desire to be hands on in anything they are involved in. People who are concerned about the environment, for example, are seldom happy with simply writing a check; instead, they want to go out into the field and plant trees, rescue animals, improve habitats, post on social media, and take their place in a protest. Likewise, with missions, when people truly grasp that there is great need and opportunity in the world and that God is calling for workers, they will want to be involved.

In finding ways regarding how to be more involved in world missions, let me suggest a few things. First, don't stop being involved in your own neighborhood or our city. We have learned that people who serve as international workers must be people who have shown themselves as evangelists in their own context.

Second, do not minimize the active role of prayer. It is through the prayers of thousands of God's people that the strongholds of Satan are being breeched around the world. Missionary work is not a sociological project; it is a supernatural assault on the kingdom of darkness.

Third, you can become involved directly by actually participating in various projects alongside of the international workers that you know. Alliance missions have moved beyond thinking of short-term missions as "make work projects." Alliance churches now send teams who travel in and out of countries, bringing with them expertise in areas such as medicine, business skills, information technology, etc.; they host week long camps for children and actively share Christ. Churches that do these are not third parties in missions. They are true participants, and as they engage the world, they find their engagement in their own city becoming even more powerful. I hope that this helps direct your passion a bit. Thanks, Wanda.

Andrew

Pastor Andrew,

In our church, we only seem to emphasize Alliance missions. Why does the Alliance just want us to support Alliance missions? Aren't we being "global" and "co-operative" by supporting many missions?

Graham

Hi Graham,

It is true that we do emphasize the work of our family of churches. However, it is not because we do not recognize that there are many great missions out there that are doing incredible work. Also, Alliance churches do support other missions, especially when there are people who received their missionary vision and call while growing up in a local Alliance church but who now serve with another group. Of course, their home church is going to continue to stand with them, as they should, in every way. But people in Alliance churches need to recognize their unique obligation to the Alliance mission. There are two ways that missions can be funded. One is by workers going out and raising their own money. This process, sometimes called "faith missions," is followed by a large number of mission organizations. However, the Alliance wished to guarantee a certain level of support to all our workers, as well as guarantee pastoral care and other levels of support. Thus, we decided that Alliance churches would put money into a pool, and out of that pool all of our missionaries would be cared for. Thus, if a local church fails in this obligation to the extent that the pool is diminished, and we cannot support our workers, then our ability to carry the message throughout the world is likewise diminished. The only source of funding our Alliance work (and workers) has is the constituency of Alliance churches that sponsor that work. What is happening, and anything that we hope can happen in the future, is predicated on the generosity and commitment of Alliance people supporting the work of our international personnel. So, support the Alliance family and then, out of a God-given generosity, support others as well. Thanks Graham!

Andrew

Andrew,

In your message, you placed a good deal of emphasis on defending North Americans and Europeans going to other countries/cultures with the message of Christianity. But in reality, isn't there a growing worldwide movement where many other countries are also sending missionaries abroad? In fact, is it not true that the future of missions may lay in non-North American countries sending people out?

Sharon

Sharon,

That's a good point. In fact, Christianity has grown hugely in what is called "the global south" (Africa, South America, etc.), while at the same time, church attendance have shrunk drastically in North America and Europe. South Korea now sends out more missionaries than any other country on earth. So, missions is no longer carried simply by North Americans, but nonetheless, the objection that missions is simply a cultural imperialism of Europe and North America is still leveled on occasion, and so I felt like it needed to be addressed in the message. Thanks for noting the changing reality Sharon; your comment/question is helpful.

Andrew

QUESTIONS FOR FURTHER CONSIDERATION
AND DISCUSSION: "PROCLAIMING JESUS"

Do you think that it is appropriate to try and influence people to change their religion? Is the statement that "engaging in this kind of endeavor is just going to create more problems" accurate?

Are people really "not okay"? Is there really a need in people's lives to know Jesus? If not, why not? If so, why so?

What is "good" about the good news of the gospel? What aspects of it offer hope and help to people in the world today?

How have you seen the church make a difference in places where you have lived or visited?

What is the relationship between "good words" and "good deeds" in the mission of the church? In other words, what role does doing good deeds play in the overall mission of the church? Is it enough? Can good works proclaim the gospel effectively? Should verbal proclamation be given priority at all times? What role does verbal proclamation play in sharing the good news?

How can your church best participate in mission today both locally and internationally?

Biblical texts to consider: Gen 3:1–9, Matt 9:9–13; 28:18–20, 2 Cor 5:11–21

Appendix

Healing Seminar

INTRODUCTION

WHEN CHURCH LEADERS BECOME aware that someone is really sick, their first response should be to pray for that person, because we believe that God cares for our entire being as humans. He cares for the brokenness and suffering of our body, mind, and spirit, and we believe that he can and does bring us healing. As Christians, we should not be left alone to hurt, for we are to live together and experience healing together as a church, which is why we are instructed to ask others to pray for us, specifically, to call for the elders, representing the church as a whole, to pray for us.

As an elder, when I receive a request to pray for a sick person, what do I do? I will admit that sometimes I worry with questions like how do I approach someone who has asked for prayer for healing, what if I do it wrong, will God still heal them, and do I have enough faith to trust God for healing?

THE PRINCIPLE OF MERCY

There are best practices in praying for the sick, and we will talk about them. But as we begin, let us focus on this one big truth: God has mercy on us in Jesus Christ. It is Jesus, our healer, who looked at the crowds and had compassion on them and healed their sickness (Matt 14:14). Even today, right now, he looks on us with compassion, and we can come to him, our shepherd, to ask for healing.

Understanding and believing in the mercy and compassion of Christ is the key to healing. We might think that certain words need to be said, or the anointing or the laying on of hands need to be done in a particular way, in order to demonstrate our faith. But actually, it is the presence of faith itself that is critical, for having faith simply means that we believe in Jesus who told us that he cares and that he is able to heal us.

As soon as I say the word "faith," another set of questions may pop into your mind. What does it mean to have faith? And perhaps as important, what does it mean not to have faith? And in between those questions, are there levels of faith, and is a certain level of faith needed for God to intervene? That is, can one have enough or not enough faith to be healed? And finally, someone may ask, do I need to show my faith in a particular or perhaps dramatic way?

Jesus said that if we pray with faith the size of a mustard seed, great things can happen as a result. See that mountain? Your faith can move it! Christians have understood that there are certain times in our lives when there are mountains that need to be moved, and sickness is one of them.

Do you believe that Jesus wants to heal and that he is able to do it? Perhaps you doubt that Jesus wants to heal, that is, you wonder if it is God's will to heal. True, there are times when God decides that we are to bear a certain illness. However, the apostle Paul tells us that he went to the Lord and asked for deliverance from an illness more than once. He only stopped when the Lord directed him to stop.

So, begin by believing that the Lord wants to heal; move into that belief like you would move into a warm room on a cold winter's night, and stay there until you are healed or until you receive from the Lord, in some manner, a definite word that healing in this instance is not to happen.

Faith, carrying the flag of the mercy of Christ, should march boldly into the fray through prayer, asking the Lord to bring health to the sufferer. But some will think that this bold faith needs demonstration. They might counsel dramatic action, such as claiming that you are healed before the symptoms disappear, or even more radically, refusing medical help.

Let us reject such counsel. Unless we have received specific instruction from the Lord in particular situations, we should never take actions that would normally be considered to be un-wise in order to demonstrate our faith. We learn this from Jesus' rejecting the tempter's challenge to throw himself from the pinnacle of the temple, so that angels would catch him. Never hesitate to go or to take a sick person to the emergency room; never refuse to undergo surgery or any procedure intended to save a life or heal a disease. Medicines and medical care are gifts from the Lord and should be received with thanksgiving.

Remember, physicians are honored in the Bible, and the church has always considered their presence to be part of the general mercy of the Lord on all people, for even as he causes his rain to fall on the just and the unjust, he has provided helpers for our health. Not all of Christ's healing will be sudden or away from the normal healing of the body, for he has given us gifts of medicine and gifts of people trained in surgery and therapy, and it is part of our exercise of faith to turn to them and receive these gifts and to receive them in Jesus' name.

Furthermore, when we pray, we do not know God's timeline, and thus, like the ten lepers who were healed and were sent by Jesus to the priests for examination (Luke 17:14), we should only claim that we are healed, when we have been examined and declared that we are healed. Until then, we should keep our hope and faith in our heart and continue to submissively seek the Lord.

Hang on to this: healing is an act of the mercy of our heavenly Father in Jesus Christ, and brought to us in love by the Holy Spirit. His mercy is not conditioned on perfect prayer or ritual, so we should not hedge our bets, so to speak, by first approaching God with doubt, for even the leper in Matt 8:1, who submissively said, "if it be your will," was actually expressing faith. Ask for healing, and let your asking be at the same time both humble and bold as you approach the throne of grace, knowing that our high priest is there for us, inviting us to come to him in our hour of need.

THE PRAYER OF FAITH

The apostle James instructs us in Jas 5:14–17 to pray for the sick, and he reminds us of Elijah who fervently prayed for the rain to stop, and the rain stopped, and then he prayed again for rain, and rain came. James tells us to pray with this kind of intensity and to pray for the sick with warm and meaningful prayers, that is, prayers of faith (Jas 5:17, 18).

What then is the prayer of faith that the apostle James calls for in Jas 5:15, the kind of prayer Elijah had when he prayed that it would not rain? We should present with all our heart our petition for healing, leaning into the prayer with our emotion, heart, and mind, but not demanding from God and not thinking that if we pray hard enough or long enough, or do some special thing, such as "take authority," that God will be compelled to heal. But we need to come as a child to our Father, as a friend to our friend Jesus, as an empty vessel to be filled by the Holy Spirit. What we want above all is to have Jesus come to the person, to the pain, and to the brokenness, and as he comes, we ask him to touch once again with his healing hand.

You may ask if this enough. Many times it is enough. Jesus comes and heals, perhaps instantly, perhaps over some days, but there is healing. But, sometimes we are called to persevere in prayer and to keep on praying without growing weary in prayer. Remember this: do not stop asking for healing, unless the Lord tells you that healing will not be forthcoming, but also do not continue to pray in a manner that seems to erode your faith rather than build it up, as this can happen when we insist that God act in the way we want him to act and on the timeline that we have laid out.

When praying for someone looking to be healed, do not offer a prayer and then forget about them, wishing them God's blessings and then hurrying off to other pressing business. No, take their burden on yourself, carry them as the friends carried the crippled man to the rooftop, and then continue to set them before Jesus, even as the friends lowered him through the hole down before the Lord (Mark 2:4). Take their need with you, and make it part of your daily prayer life. Be strong and persistent but humble, this is one of the marks of faith.

On the part of the person who is sick, what faith does this person need? Yes, the sick also need faith. The apostle Paul looked into the crowd at Lystra and saw a man whom he discerned had faith to be healed. The very act of coming for prayer demonstrates faith, but also when we are sick, we should not be thinking that we are owed healing or that God must prove himself to us, but be waiting quietly for his merciful touch.

A final trap must be addressed, that is, when healing occurs after we have prayed. In this circumstance, we may be tempted to feel proud, because our prayers have produced a miracle. Perhaps, goes the quiet whisper, it is because we really do have great faith and a great anointing, or perhaps there is great favor. If you happen to hear such diabolical words in your mind, ever so soft as they may be spoken, remember this: your role in this part of the great drama of salvation is as incidental as a stagehand who carried on a small chair as the scene is changed. God needed someone to do a small job, you were available, and you did it, which is good, but not really praiseworthy, so give Christ glory and mean it.

HEALING HAPPENS WITHIN COMMUNITY

It pleases the Lord to show his presence and power to unbelievers through signs and wonders. But, within the community of believers, the practice of the oneness of the body of Christ is the environment in which the Lord ministers to his children. This is why the apostle James instructs us that, when we are sick, we are to call for the leaders of the church to anoint the sick with oil and pray for them. We are also to call for them for the confession of sins. The elders are there as representatives of the whole congregation, which through them, is lifting up the afflicted.

We should never think of ourselves as living alone before God, but always as living in a holy community, a city set apart; and when we suffer, the church in some way also suffers, and when Christ shows mercy, the whole church experiences his mercy. Pastors and elders should continually work to develop the church's faith by teaching the congregation to have an attitude of expecting God to act and show mercy, and to bring glory to Christ. This should be done by studying healing in the Scriptures.

Focus on the explicit instructions of the apostle James in James 5. But there are also other passages on healing throughout the Bible.[1] Find them, learn them, and teach them to others. As part of this teaching ministry, be familiar with some of the stories of healing throughout church history. John Bunyan prayed for his wife when she went into early labor, and the contractions ceased; Spurgeon was prayed over by his deacons and was healed. There are many such testimonies that the Lord uses to strengthen us as we approach him. Thus, just as acts of healing are recorded for us, acts of healing in the congregation should be shared with the congregation.

While teaching and encouraging, give opportunity for people to respond to healing. After the communion service is an excellent time to invite people to come for anointing, for people have contemplated the Lord and his love and have confessed their sins. Also consider other opportunities, such as retreats for youth, women, and men, where people can quietly seek the Lord and focus on him. Don't leave out weekly and monthly meetings, such as small groups, men's and women's meetings and special seminars, for all these occasions present an opportunity to point people to Jesus the great physician.

---

1. For example, Gen 20:17; 25:21; Exod 15:26; 2 Chr 30:20; Ps 30:2; 107:20; Isa 53:5. In the New Testament, other than the amazing miracles of Jesus, healing passages can be found in Acts 4:9; 5:16; 8:7; 14:9; 28:8.

THE MOMENT OF PRAYER AND ANOINTING

An invitation is given, and people do respond. What should the leaders do next? First, be sure to make everyone feel comfortable. They may be kneeling, but can they kneel for very long? Make sure to be sensitive to their needs. Provide for their physical needs, so that they are not distressed, especially if it is obvious that they have an injury. If those who are coming forward are not familiar to the people gathered to minister to them, introduce yourselves and then ask the person to simply state their prayer request, and respectfully listen to them quietly, while affirming that you understand what is being requested. Give verbal assurance to the person that Christ loves them and cares for them and that he is the one who has invited them forward to cast all their cares on him.

And, while doing these things, listen to the Holy Spirit who may be giving you a word of knowledge regarding the seeker. Perhaps there is a sin that needs to be confessed, or, perhaps the prayer for healing should encompass even more than what the seeker has expressed. Perhaps a word of instruction or even a rebuke must be administered and an agreement for life change reached before prayer can be effectual. Let that happen. And if the prayer is after a communion service, then there has been a time for confession offered. If not, we should ask if there are any unconfessed sin, and if there is, the person seeking healing should take this moment to confess any sins to the Lord.

When these words of ministry and moments of listening have been accomplished, it is time to anoint and pray. Put a small drop of oil on your finger and apply it to the person's forehead, usually making a cross, which again puts the focus on the Lord. Say, " . . . (name) . . . I anoint you in the name of the Father, and of the Son, and of the Holy Spirit," and then begin a prayer for healing.

When you pray, invite Christ to come, confessing your own helplessness and acknowledging his all sufficiency. Bring the sick person before the Lord. You might even experience the Spirit giving you a picture in your mind of one of the New Testament scenes, where people brought their friends to Jesus, and you might mention that mental picture in your prayer, for it is from the Lord. I have had pictures from Scripture come to me as I prayed for healing (e.g. the woman touching the hem of Jesus' garment; the friends lowering the lame man through the roof). Thus, I will sometimes pray a few words, such as "just as the men lowered the lame man through the roof we bring . . . Name . . . to you today," or "just as you healed the woman who touched the hem of your garment we bring . . . Name . . . to you today."

Be sure to specifically name the illness or distress that needs healing, and specifically ask for healing. Pray that, if there is a disease, that it will be removed; and if there is ongoing medical treatment, such as an impending surgery, that the treatment will be empowered by Christ, and the physician, surgeons, and nurses will be guided and given the skill for the surgery. Then, close the prayer by coming directly to Christ; ask for the life-giving resurrection power of Jesus to come into the person's body and for this person to be restored to robust health, so that Christ might be honored and his name exalted. And finally, close with a hearty Amen that signifies your faith.

CONCLUSION

As the body of Christ, the church looks to the Holy Spirit to bring all the wonders of Jesus to her; she lives in the heavenly places with Christ and expects to experience his care and his gifts in this life. Let us call on Jesus to come to us in our church and show his love, mercy, and care to us in our infirmities. Call on him with faith for one another, and do not grow weary, casting all our cares on him, for he cares for us.

Bibliography

Green, Joel. *1 Peter*. The Two Horizons New Testament Commentary. Grand Rapids: Eerdmans, 2007.

McCartney, Dan. *James*. Baker Exegetical Commentary on the New Testament. Grand Rapids: Baker, 2009.

Middleton, Richard. *A New Heaven and a New Earth: Reclaiming Biblical Eschatology*. Grand Rapids: Baker, 2014.

Muck, Terry, and Frances S. Adeney. *Christianity Encountering World Religions: The Practice of Mission in the Twenty-First Century*. Grand Rapids: Baker, 2009.

Niklaus, Robert L., et. al. *All for Jesus: God at Work in the Christian and Missionary Alliance over One Hundred Years*. Camp Hill, PA: Christian Publications, 1986.

Patterson, James, and Peter Kim. *The Day America Told the Truth: What People Really Believed about Everything That Matters*. New York: Prentice-Hall, 1991.

Smith, Christian, and Patricia Snell. *Souls in Transition: The Religious and Spiritual Lives of Emerging Adults*. New York: Oxford University Press, 2009.

Stoesz, Samuel J. *Understanding My Church: A Profile of the Christian and Missionary Alliance*. Camp Hill, PA: Christian Publications, 1988.

Tozer, A. W. *Wingspread: A. B. Simpson: A Study in Spiritual Altitude*. Harrisburg, PA: Christian Publications, 1943.

Wright, N. T. *Surprised by Hope: Rethinking Heaven, the Resurrection and the Mission of the Church*. New York: HarperCollins, 2009.

Printed in the USA
CPSIA information can be obtained
at www.ICGtesting.com
LVHW010426280923
759516LV00004B/291

9 781498 294744